TRACING YOUR LABOUR MOVEMENT ANCESTORS

TRACING YOUR LABOUR MOVEMENT ANCESTORS

MARK CRAIL

Pen & Sword
FAMILY HISTORY

First published in Great Britain in 2009 by
PEN & SWORD FAMILY HISTORY
an imprint of
Pen & Sword Books Ltd
47 Church Street
Barnsley
South Yorkshire
S70 2AS

ISBN 978 1 84884 059 1

A CIP catalogue record for this book is available from the British Library.

Printed and bound in England by
CPI UK

Pen & Sword Books Ltd incorporates the imprints of
Pen & Sword Aviation, Pen & Sword Maritime, Pen & Sword Military,
Wharncliffe Local History, Pen and Sword Select, Pen and Sword Military Classics,
Leo Cooper, Remember When, Seaforth Publishing and Frontline Publishing.

For a complete list of Pen & Sword titles please contact
PEN & SWORD BOOKS LIMITED
47 Church Street, Barnsley, South Yorkshire, S70 2AS, England
E-mail: enquiries@pen-and-sword.co.uk
Website: www.pen-and-sword.co.uk

CONTENTS

PREFACE

Trade unions are among the largest membership bodies in the country. Even after thirty years of decline, they can still claim nearly eight million members, making them vastly bigger than the RSPCA or Women's Institute, and twice the size of the National Trust. But two centuries ago even to join such an organization was illegal, and to swear the oath required of new members or to engage in 'combinations' to demand higher pay could result in a harsh prison sentence or transportation to the colonies.

The history of the labour movement encompasses lockouts, strikes, demonstrations and sometimes a revolutionary commitment to building a different society. But it is mainly the story of our ancestors' working lives. The issues with which trade unions have dealt encompass wages, working conditions, mutual support and friendship. Before the welfare state, the friendly society benefits that trade unions offered were an essential safety net for those who fell on hard times. The branch structure provided a social network not just for those in work but for the retired members, who often received a pension from their unions. And they gave ordinary people a voice in government policies.

The labour movement has always had a strong sense of its own history. The creation myths of the old craft unions now form merely a colourful prelude to accounts of later membership growth, while the initiation ceremonies of the early nineteenth century are regarded as quaint or embarrassing aberrations on the part of the movement's pioneers. But the bureaucratic frame of mind required to build and maintain union structures over many years has ensured the survival of records that can help family historians to piece together the lives of ancestors who would otherwise have left little documentary evidence.

In writing these opening paragraphs, I am already acutely aware that I have seemed to use the terms trade union movement and labour movement interchangeably. In fact, although the trade unions are at its heart, the labour movement itself is a wider if rather fuzzily defined entity whose precise boundaries have long been the source of much disagreement.

Within the labour movement will undoubtedly be found the Labour Party – which was in part set up by and has been substantially funded for more than a century by the trade unions. The now defunct Communist Party of Great Britain with its strong industrial base and close ties to the unions also has a good claim to be considered a part of the wider labour movement. From there on, things become less certain. What of the many other left-wing parties that rose and fell over the twentieth century – from the Second World War dissidents of Common Wealth to the explosion of Trotskyist groups in the 1960s and 1970s? To some extent I have included these as they are unlikely to be covered in many other family history books. The same applies to the cultural and social groups – from Clarion cycling clubs to Labour churches – that grew up organically within the labour movement.

I have, however, drawn the line at attempting to track the hundreds of single-issue campaigns from the Peace Pledge Union to the Campaign for Nuclear Disarmament, the Anti-Nazi League to the Anglo-Soviet Friendship Society. Although labour movement organizations played key roles in establishing and running many of these groups, they were from the start intended to be wider than or even separate from the parties that spawned them – either from a genuine intent to build a broad coalition in support of their cause, or in some cases to become front organizations for their parent bodies, useful tools to extend political influence in a sometimes dubious manner.

My own association with the labour movement began in 1979 when, with monumentally bad timing, I joined the Labour Party just as millions were deserting it and the best part of a generation of Conservative government was about to begin. A year later I became a member of the National Union of Journalists, just as trade union membership hit its historic high and began a precipitous and apparently inexorable decline.

My interest in family history took another twenty-five years to develop, but when I began my research I was delighted to discover that family tradition was correct and we did, indeed, have an active Chartist in our midst. Alas, James Grassby, my great-great-great-grandfather, was no better in his political timing than me. After serving the movement for more than a decade in a variety of roles, he became general secretary of the National Charter Association in 1851. Soon afterwards, the organization imploded, leaving James and his fellow members of the executive to pay off its substantial debts.

Since James was followed by a number of generations who eschewed the labour movement and rose to local prominence in the Conservative Party and freemasonry instead, I can boast no other family ties to trade union and labour politics. Even so, I find myself fascinated by the organizational history of the labour movement, its mergers, splits and schisms, and by its rich visual culture of banners, badges, memorabilia and ephemera.

ARRANGEMENT OF THIS BOOK

The book is arranged in ten chapters. It begins with a guide to the types of record you may encounter while researching a labour movement ancestor and introduces some of the principal archives for this type of material. Where full contact information for an archive has been included in Chapter 1, I have not repeated it elsewhere in the book.

There are then four chapters dealing chronologically with the history of trade unions over the past two centuries. The experiences of individual trade unionists during each of these periods will, of course, have been incredibly diverse, depending on their trade, location, the prevailing economic conditions at any particular time, and of course the depth of their involvement in trade unionism. Nonetheless, I have tried to illustrate some of this by selecting a couple of real individuals in each period and briefly telling their life story.

The three chapters which follow trace the development of the political work of the labour movement, dealing in turn with Chartism, the Labour Party and its forebears, and the Communist Party of Great Britain and other left-wing parties. A further chapter introduces some of the many social and cultural organizations that have grown out of the labour movement, from cycling clubs to socialist Sunday schools. The main body of the book concludes with a short chapter on the development of the electoral franchise since 1832 and suggests how electoral registers and related records might also help you to trace your labour movement ancestor.

Many websites are cited in this book. Since websites are dynamic entities, the URL (= Uniform Resource Locator, the web address) may change. All those cited in this book were correct at the time of going to press. If a URL has changed, the web page may simply have been moved to another location on the same site, and it should be possible to find the web page by searching on the main website. If a website has changed address, it should be possible to find it by using an internet search engine.

ACKNOWLEDGEMENTS

Simon Fowler, the editor of *Ancestors* magazine, published my earliest forays into writing for family historians and talked me into writing this book. He made many helpful suggestions for improvements and additions. Lynette Cawthra and her colleagues at the Working Class Movement Library in Salford have been unfailingly helpful in providing information on obscure causes and people. Chris Coates, librarian of the TUC Library Collections at London Metropolitan University, has been generous in dealing with my queries and requests for help. My partner Adèle and son Tom made time and space on the family computer to allow me to research and write this book. My thanks to them all. Any factual errors or political judgements with which you disagree are, of course, entirely down to me.

Chapter 1

UNDERSTANDING LABOUR
MOVEMENT RECORDS

'A trade union, as we understand the term, is a continuous association of wage-earners for the purpose of maintaining or improving the conditions of their working lives.' This definition, offered by the Fabian intellectuals Sidney and Beatrice Webb as the opening sentence in their *History of Trade Unionism* in 1890, remains the best and most enduring summary of the role and purpose of trade unions yet written.

It is the very fact of their being 'continuous associations' – organizations which endure and continue in existence over years if not decades – and the role that they have played in improving the working lives of millions of ordinary people over the past two centuries that make trade unions such a potentially valuable source of information for family historians.

The wider labour movement, unlike trade unions, may lack a similarly concise definition. But who could not fail to be fascinated and want to find out more about an ancestor involved in the Chartist struggles of the 1840s, the rise of Victorian socialist societies in the 1880s, or the creation of the Labour Party and its rise to power in the twentieth century?

Getting Started

As with all family history research, you should first write down what you know. Ask around among family members about the working lives of the ancestors you wish to research. Most people will have spent the majority of their waking day at work for anything up to forty or fifty years, and their social networks will often have included workmates and those in the same trades. Trade unions were a central part of work and social experience for millions of people, and any trace of that life that can be rescued from the historical record casts new light on what we know of our ancestors.

There are known to have been more than 5,000 trade unions in the UK alone over the past 200 years. Many were small organizations – confined to a single district, town or even factory – and short-lived. Some never grew beyond a membership numbered in double figures, and often all evidence of their existence had disappeared but for passing mentions in other records.

Today, mergers and amalgamations, changing social attitudes, and the decline of once mighty industries have reduced the number of trade unions known to be in existence to just 185. At the turn of the twentieth century, however, there were at least 1,300 trade unions vying for members in what was then a far less regulated and consequently often far more confrontational world of work.

As a consequence, even tracking down the correct union to research can be a time-consuming and sometimes frustrating task. It is, however, essential. A late nineteenth-century London cabinetmaker, for example, might have joined the Cabinet Makers' Society. But depending on their specific location and line of work, there was also an East End Cabinet Makers' Association, a Hebrew Cabinet Makers' Union (organizing mostly immigrant Jewish workers), a London Society of Cabinet Makers (which may be another name for the London West End Cabinet Makers' Association), and an Alliance Cabinet Makers' Association to choose from. And since people often used descriptive names rather than the proper names of unions, there is ample scope for confusion.

It is also worth bearing in mind that, although your ancestor may well have worked in trades where trade unions were organized, they might themselves never have joined up.

You may be lucky. Your ancestor may have been sufficiently prominent to be included in the *Dictionary of Labour Biography*, a decades-long project which so far runs to twelve volumes of researched and referenced biographical entries on trade unionists and other activists on the political left. Otherwise, the task of tracking down any surviving records of your ancestor's involvement in the trade union and labour movement involves a process of narrowing the search to as tight a set of variables as possible – even if in part this may include some guesswork and judicious backtracking from research dead-ends.

Step one: establish as precisely as possible what exactly your ancestor did for a living. As a weaver, did they work in cotton, poplin or silk? Did they weave material for use in clothes, ribbons or furniture? Did they actually weave or were they an overseer? All of these groups had different unions at one time or another. Often, too, there were separate but parallel unions for men and women in the same trades.

Step two: pin down the locations in which your ancestor worked. Although by the middle of the nineteenth century some unions were national in scope and were beginning to evolve central organization and record-keeping, others remained highly localized through to the end of the twentieth century. Printworkers and weavers, to give but two examples, often organized in bewilderingly small localities, while even after the establishment of the Miners' Federation of Great Britain in 1888 (and subsequently the National Union of Mineworkers in 1945), constituent areas and even lodges maintained considerable autonomy.

Step three: work out when your ancestor would have been working and might have been a trade union member. There is nothing more frustrating than to track down the existence of a Manchester Operative Fishmongers and Poulterers Association only to discover that it was not founded until the mid-1870s, by which time your fish-selling ancestor was long dead.

Step four: having established where and when your ancestor was working and precisely what they did, find out what unions might have been open to them. This book aims to help you with step four, and to go beyond that by suggesting records that might survive to reveal otherwise lost details of your ancestor's involvement in the trade union and labour movement.

Tracking Down the Right Union

Once you have completed steps one to three and are ready to begin on step four, it will of course help if you already have some evidence of the union to which your ancestor belonged – a badge or membership card, perhaps if they were sufficiently actively involved a mention in a published labour movement history, or possibly an elderly relative's memories.

If not, a good place to start is the Trade Union Ancestors website (http://www.unionancestors.co.uk), a central feature of which is an A to Z index of known trade unions. By searching here, you should be able to compile a shortlist of union names worthy of further investigation. Be careful, however, to ensure that the search terms you use are sufficiently widely drawn. When looking for a shoemaker, include shoemakers, cobblers, cloggers, bootmakers and cordwainers.

Armed with this shortlist, you should now consult the *Historical Directory of Trade Unions*. This encyclopaedic work, begun in 1980, now runs to five volumes, with a sixth promised for 2009. Organized by industry, the directory provides single-paragraph histories of each union mentioned, giving, where possible, formation dates, alternative names, the fate of the union and sources. Where little is known, these entries may be very brief. The entry for the London Plumbers' Society, for example, reads:

> Formed in 1904 with twenty-eight members, the Society had only fifteen members in 1910. The secretary from 1913 was J Groves, of Elgin Avenue, Paddington. It went out of existence in 1916.
>
> Sources: BoT Reports; Certification Office; Industrial Directory of the UK.

Though hard to find, it is worthwhile tracking down the relevant volume of the *Historical Directory of Trade Unions*. There is a complete set in the library at the National Archives. More general libraries may be able to help locate a copy, but it may be necessary to approach a specialist, university library or archive. Without it, you will find it almost impossible to exclude from your research all those organizations which operated in the wrong era, did not recruit in the right part of the country, or have simply left too little evidence of their own existence.

Now that you have a manageable list of trade unions whose records are worth consulting, it is worth getting to grips with the types of record you may encounter in your research.

What Union Records Exist?

Admission books

It was not easy to join a nineteenth-century trade union. Membership was often restricted to an elite of working men who had served their apprenticeship and could be trusted by their colleagues. New members would need sponsors, there were oaths to swear, and evidence of suitable apprenticeship and employment in the relevant trade to provide. As national union structures became stronger from the 1850s onwards, records of those admitted to membership began to be assembled in head offices.

The best examples of surviving admission books (or registration books) are those produced by the Amalgamated Society of Carpenters and Joiners (from 1895), and the Friendly Society of Operative Stone Masons (from 1886). Although these vary from union to union, details typically include the new member's name, age, number of years in the trade, date admitted, their marital status, and their nominee for funeral benefit. Basic lists of members joining the Amalgamated Society of House Decorators and Painters between 1873 and 1900 also survive. All these records, and many others, can be found at Warwick University's Modern Records Centre.

Usually registers are organized by date of entry, so unless the exact year in which someone took up a trade is known for sure, searches can be time-consuming and frustrating.

Membership cards

Once admitted, a new member would be issued with their card. These were important documents, and most unions issued a new one each year, or occasionally even quarterly. Although arrangements vary, most have space to record the member's name and address, the branch to which they belong (along with details of the branch secretary), and often a membership number.

Many unions used the card to record weekly or monthly subscriptions, making it a valuable document for members seeking to prove their entitlement to benefits. This would have been especially important for workers whose jobs took them 'tramping' from town to town, and who would look to the local branch of their union for assistance. This use for membership cards evolved out of the 'blank books' issued to friendly society members as early as the

Trade union membership cards.
Source: author's collection.

eighteenth century, but survived well into the nineteenth. From the early 1840s, for example, a member of the United Society of Brushmakers with their card stamped was entitled to a night's bed, supper and a pint of beer in any town where the society maintained a 'house of call'.

Emblems and badges

The heyday of the union emblem was from 1870 to 1900. Unions produced large, ornate certificates featuring their emblems, which usually depict the work of the union's members – often with a suitably uplifting religious or secular slogan. In some unions one in three members had one on the wall of their home. In 1882, the 12,000-strong Amalgamated Society of Cotton Spinners ordered 3,000 emblems which it sold to members at 3 shillings each.

Hundreds more found their way into the upstairs rooms of public houses, which were often used as union meeting rooms. The union leader F W Galton told the historians Sidney and Beatrice Webb that pub walls were frequently decorated with trade society emblems 'interspersed with gold mirrors and advertising almanacs'.

Such emblems were seldom given away, but could be purchased from the union's head office. Writing in the 1890s, the Webbs

Trade union badges old and new. Source: author's collection.

commented that a member would usually buy his copy when he married, and it would be 'hung, gaily framed, in his front parlour'. 'To his wife it is the charter of their rights in case of sickness, want of work or death. As such it is an object of pride in the household, pointed out with due impressiveness to friends and casual visitors.'

By the early twentieth century, few new emblems were being commissioned, and as stocks of the old designs were used up, no more were printed. But badges were growing in popularity. Badges had evolved from decorative items attached to the ceremonial sashes worn by branch officials on formal occasions, but once adopted by members as a means of displaying their allegiances and a way of recognizing fellow union members, they spread widely.

The first badges in a form recognizable today – enamelled metal displaying the union's name and emblem on the front and with a pin or buttonhole attachment on the back – arrived in the 1870s, and by the end of the decade the Associated Society of Locomotive Engineers and Firemen was also producing badges that could be attached to watch chains.

By the end of the century, union symbols adorned the lapels of millions of working men and women. Special versions were – and still are – produced for branch officers, and to mark the point at which a member has clocked up ten, twenty or more years in the union. Some unions also have a tradition of producing badges for local branches or particular trade groups.

At the turn of the twentieth century, the TUC had begun to produce badges for delegates to its annual congress. This tradition continues today, each badge bearing the name of that year's president.

Commemorative badges marking notable strikes were first struck in the 1890s, and in turn the wearing of union badges has itself sometimes been the cause for industrial action. London bus workers in 1913, nurses in 1918 and 'tea shop girls' at J Lyons & Co. corner houses in 1920 all walked out after members were dismissed for wearing their union badges on their uniforms. Even into the twenty-first century, there have been similar confrontations in the Prison Service and on the railways.

Anyone lucky enough to have a union membership card, badge or emblem belonging to a family member has not just a personal memento of that individual but a crucial step on the road to finding out more about them – clear evidence of the union to which they belonged, and perhaps even some indication of branch offices they held.

UNDERSTANDING TRADE UNION EMBLEMS: THE GENERAL UNION OF CARPENTERS AND JOINERS

Victorian trade union emblems were rich in imagery, often drawing on biblical sources and other religious references and classical allusions. Few were more ornate and packed with messages than that of the General Union of Carpenters and Joiners (see illustration).

The General Union had been founded in 1827 and in its early days counted its members in the hundreds. By 1860, it claimed 3,821 members, but was facing strong competition from the rival Amalgamated Society of Carpenters and Joiners. Against this background, in 1864 members of the Bolton Lodge suggested that the General Union should have its own emblem, and adverts were placed in local and labour movement newspapers offering a prize of £7 for the best design.

Members were issued with the first emblems, at a size of 24 inches by 18 inches, in 1866, along with a booklet and line drawing explaining its key elements. At the centre of this highly ornate emblem,

> between and partly beneath the luxuriant branches of the Noble Oak is situate the Design, representing staircases, palisadings, numerous figures, landscapes, symbolisms, maxims, proverbs, &c, and an ornamental building with various spires, pinnacles, and arches, that rise in picturesque beauty from among the young ash that spread their foliage through its many crevices and unique towers. This building is raised completely and exclusively by the art of Carpentry and Joinery, to exhibit a specimen of our workmanship, and to show the beauty of a timber edifice.

On the pillar to the left is the cardinal virtue Hope, to the right is Justice. Next to Hope is a carpenter 'with bass and tools in one hand and trying plane under his arm', his expression intended to evoke that of Joseph. He is shown conversing with 'the modern and manly-looking joiner', with a saw in one hand and compass in the other.

Other symbols in the emblem include the figures of Peace, Plenty, Reason, Holiness and Resignation. Fortitude holds a compass 'indicating the aid of science in supporting and strengthening the mind', and rests against Industry. On each side of the building is a workshop in which carpenters and joiners ply their trades, while over the central doorway are the tools of their trades. A rose, shamrock and thistle entwined in the bottom corners represent the United Kingdom, and at the top of the design the 'Allseeing Eye of the Omnipotent King of kings' (a Masonic symbol) looks down and diffuses rays of glory on all beneath.

Whether or not the emblem helped, the General Union of Carpenters and Joiners managed to survive in a competitive union world, and could claim 9,000 members by 1900. It eventually merged with its main rival in 1921 to form the Amalgamated Society of Woodworkers.

The General Union of Carpenters and Joiners' mid-nineteenth-century emblem.

Membership lists

Membership lists differ from admission registers in that they name all members at a particular date. The survival of these records has been patchy, and the largest repository of trade union records in the UK – the Modern Records Centre at Warwick University – does not usually collect them.

However, it does make exceptions for lists of particular interest. For example, it has a copy of a multi-volume register compiled by the Amalgamated Society of Railway Servants in 1897 listing all current members and all new members who joined thereafter. Those who joined before 1897 are arranged chronologically by year of joining and then in rough alphabetical order by branch. Those who joined from 1897 onwards are arranged purely chronologically. The register has the name, age, date of joining, occupation, railway company, branch, and sometimes dates of branch transfers, retirement and death. But there is no index, so a search will require either the member's number or their exact date of joining and branch.

Most large unions simply did not attempt to maintain a current register of all members as it would have been impractical to keep up-to-date lists of tens of thousands of individuals. Although lists would have been kept by branches, many have not survived or are scattered in local archives and national collections. The London Borough of Hackney's archive department, for example, holds some membership records for local branches of upholsterers', electricians' and woodworkers' trade unions, while the Tyne and Wear archives department has records from the United Pattern Makers' Association's Jarrow branch.

Some unions had no effective central membership register as late as the 1980s, when they were made necessary by the introduction of new laws by the then Conservative government compelling unions to carry out postal ballots of members for industrial action and to elect certain officials.

Minute books and branch records

Minute taking is more or less a core part of trade union culture. Records of who attends, any offices they hold, and to at least some extent the contribution they make to the meeting are made at all levels, from the smallest branch committees to the most powerful national executives. Where anything other than a cobbled together collection of

IN MEMORIAM.

Branch.	Name	Date of Death.	Age	Disease.	How long a Member.		Amount of Funeral Allowance.		
		1905.	Yrs.		Years.	Months.	£	s.	d.
Accrington	J. W. B. Bell	Sept. 25	46	Valvular Heart Disease ..	8	7	10	0	0
„	M. Keenan	Dec. 25	31	Pneumonia	0	6	5	0	0
Burnley No. 1......	W. Starkie	Jan. 23	44	Cerebral Hemorrhage	9	0	10	0	0
„	W. Machin	„ 28	51	Blood Poisoning.........	10	0	10	0	0
„	J. Cardall.............	May 12	19	Valvular Disease of Heart..	2	9	7	0	0
„	M. Batty	Dec. 15	47	Cerebral Hemorrhage	8	11	7	0	0
Bradford	M. Hartley	Aug. 12	29	Bronchitis	3	1	7	0	0
Bolton	W. Wilson	April 10	69	Senile Decay	15	0	7	0	0
Blackburn No. 1....	J. Brown	Jan. 9	46	Pneumonia	8	0	7	0	0
„	R. Winder	Feb. 22	44	Cardiac Failure	6	0	7	0	0
„	J. Lowe	Mar. 21	48	Syncope, Pneumonia......	10	0	10	0	0
„	J. Brennan	Sept. 9	64	Heart Failure...........	12	0	7	0	0
Cardiff	W. Tripp	May 15	57	Heart Disease	8	8	10	0	0
„	G. H. Beavan	June 9	43	Organic Disease of Brain...	6	9	10	0	0
„	C. Rudd	Nov. 29	46	Phthisis, Exhaustion	2	6	7	0	0
Edinburgh	J. Stout	„ 21	30	Phthisis Pulmonalis	1	1	7	0	0
Halifax No. 1	J. Mitchell	Mar. 18	72	Cardiac Disease	10	0	7	0	0
Huddersfield No. 1..	W. Inman	June 11	63	Cerebral Apoplexy	13	8	10	0	0
Huddersfield No. 2..	J. Langfield............	Jan. 26	68	Softening of Brain........	12	11	7	0	0
„ ..	A. Cartwright	„ 29	66	Hemiplegia	4	6	7	0	0
„ ..	J. Brook	April 17	47	Heart Failure	8	1	10	0	0
„ ..	J. A. Hopkinson	„ 17	38	Typhoid Fever	4	9	7	0	0
						Car. fwd.	176	0	0

The Amalgamated Association of Tramway and Vehicle Workers' annual report for 1905 records the deaths of members and the sums paid in funeral allowances.
Source: author's collection.

journals and personal possessions exist, union archives tend to hold minute books in abundance.

Trade unions were particularly anxious to ensure that members' money was spent wisely and that those members who fell on hard times were given the support to which they were entitled. Branch records will usually scrupulously record payments made to members who were unable to work through sickness or unemployment, those given support during strikes and those granted money to travel or emigrate in search of work. Many unions also provided death benefits for members and (since most members of most unions were men) their wives.

By the twentieth century, many union branches used carbon books for correspondence, writing the letter on a top sheet which could be torn out and posted while retaining the bottom copy for the branch's records. Though most of these have long since been lost or destroyed, some can be found in specialist union archives or lodged in local records offices.

Branch returns and annual reports

Union branches were expected to keep their head office fully informed of all their activities. Formal returns were required monthly, quarterly or at least annually, depending on the individual union's rules. These returns would include lists of new members and those in receipt of benefits, along with details of the branch accounts.

Information from branch returns would feed into the production of the national union's annual report – a document frequently running to hundreds of pages. Although this will often be of limited help to family historians except as an aid to understanding the union's general activities, most contain lists of branch officials – sometimes only branch secretaries, but in other cases chairs, treasurers and possibly auditors – and their addresses. Some unions' annual reports provide much information, however: those of the London Society of Compositors from 1886 to 1922, for example, list superannuation allowances, funeral allowances, removal grants, and unemployed claimants.

Union journals

By the early years of the twentieth century, most larger unions produced a monthly circular for members to keep them up to date, record benefit payments, note new collective agreements with employers and report on the state of trade in different towns. Some unions were already producing regular publications for members at a much earlier date. *The Stonemasons' Fortnightly Circular*, for example, first appeared in 1834 and constitutes an immensely important record of trade union activity, including statistical and other information about the Friendly Society of Operative Stone Masons along with more

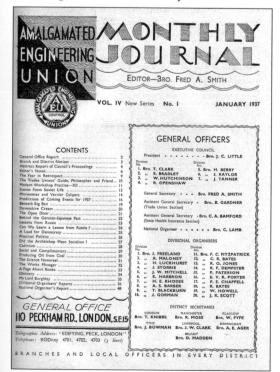

The Amalgamated Engineering Union's monthly journal for January 1937. Source: author's collection.

general reports on the building trade and wider labour movement.

Over the years, these circulars were to develop into newspapers and magazines. Today, of course, they are usually supplemented by union websites. Journals are an invaluable source of information, often carrying lists of those who have come to the attention of the union, as benefit claimants, or local record holders – or to record their expulsion and warn branches against having anything to do with them. And they could be surprisingly explicit in the information they gave, reporting, for example, the details of an injured member's accident and medical report, as well as the compensation paid to them.

Union journals also became increasingly a forum for internal debate, as an account quoted by the trade union historians Sidney and Beatrice Webb noted, with 'letters from lodges or from individual members on all sorts of topics, including spicy abuse of the Central Executive, and tart rejoinders from the General Secretary'.

Union histories

The first union histories began to appear in the early years of the twentieth century. Although most are long out of print, even old and obscure titles can often be found in second-hand bookshops and on websites such as ABE Books (http://www.abebooks.co.uk) for a few pounds.

Most are 'official' histories, sponsored and often published by the unions whose stories they tell. Although this can undermine their objectivity, the authors are usually more than able to compensate through unrivalled access to decades' worth of original records and personal sources.

Typically, union histories fall into two types: those written by retired union officials who have lived through many of the events they describe; and the generally more recent accounts researched and written by specialist historians. At worst a union history book will give an insight into the industry in which its members worked, the efforts they made to improve their lives through the union, and some idea of the main characters. Beyond that it is possible to hope that an ancestor may put in an appearance through their involvement in a conference or dispute – and may even be recognizable from one of the formal photographs of the union's early executives.

Although it is impossible in a book of this length to list all published union histories, a selection is included in the Further Reading section.

The official record

The Trade Union Act of 1871 gave the Registrar of Friendly Societies responsibility for maintaining a list of trade unions. Registration was not compulsory, but in practice almost all unions of any substance signed up in due course because doing so gave certain tax advantages when they paid out membership benefits. From that date until the Industrial Relations Act 1971 created the Chief Registrar of Trade Unions and Employers' Associations as a successor body, registered unions were required to submit annual returns setting out details of their main officials and of their accounts.

These records and further correspondence can be found in the National Archives in FS 7, FS 11, FS 12, FS 24, FS 25, FS 26, FS 27, FS 28, FS 29, FS 33 and FS 34, but are unlikely to contain information on individual union members other than those required to sign the annual return. Where records have survived, however, they will often give a good indication of the ways in which a union spent its money – the bulk, at least in the late nineteenth and early twentieth centuries, usually spent on sickness and death benefits, with strike pay and support for other unions accounting for smaller sums. Some were also prepared to help members make new lives overseas with a small grant.

In addition, from the 1880s onwards the Board of Trade and subsequently the Ministry of Labour collected principally statistical information on trade unions and industrial disputes. These records, including the trade disputes record books, which sought to analyze (very briefly) every strike and lockout from 1901 onwards, are also in the National Archives, in LAB 10, LAB 11, LAB 27 and LAB 34. Trade disputes record books typically record where a dispute took place, its start and finish dates, the number of workers involved, the cause of the dispute and – where possible – how it was resolved.

The Ministry of Labour was also responsible from 1914 for the Industrial Court, later known as the Arbitration Tribunals, and its records can be found in LAB 3.

Tracking Down the Records

Trade union and labour movement records are widely dispersed and many, of course, have not survived. All too often local and even national membership records have been destroyed when the organization went out of existence. Happily, labour movement history is a thriving discipline, and there are a number of specialist archives dedicated to preserving and facilitating the study of what survives. Two excellent starting points are the National Register of Archives (http://www.nationalarchives.gov.uk/nra) and the Access to Archives project (http://www.nationalarchives.gov.uk/a2a), both of which provide means of searching across local and specialist archives.

More detailed information relating to specific time periods and organizations appears in later chapters. Here, however, is an introduction to the largest and most comprehensive specialist collections. As with all proposed visits to archives and specialist libraries, it is a good idea before setting out to look on websites and phone where necessary to check on opening times, booking/ reservation requirements and any other restrictions there may be. In some cases it is necessary to get written permission from the organization concerned before consulting their archives, and more recent papers may remain closed.

Modern Records Centre

University Library, University of Warwick, Coventry CV4 7AL
Tel: 024 7652 4219
Web: http://www2.warwick.ac.uk/services/library/mrc
The Modern Records Centre houses an unrivalled selection of trade union, industrial relations and labour movement archives, including many collections donated by major trade unions nationally, regionally and locally. The union records deposited here are too many and varied to list individually, but special mention should be made of the Transport and General Workers' Union collection, which occupies 1,200 boxes and was not fully catalogued until 2008, and the TUC collection. The centre also has an extensive collection of records on local labour movements, Trotskyism and pacifism. A full list of the unions represented in the archive can be found at http://www2. warwick.ac.uk/services/library/mrc/archivecatalogues/browsepick list and choosing 'find the catalogue of a particular collection'.

Working Class Movement Library

51 The Crescent, Salford M5 4WX
Tel: 0161 736 3601
Web: http://www.wcml.org.uk
Set up by the late Ruth and Eddie Frow in their own home, the Working Class Movement Library has an extensive and eclectic

collection of material ranging from trade union membership records through to personal archives and labour movement ephemera. The Library now occupies premises in Salford and has charitable status. Its catalogue is available online, along with general descriptive lists of a great deal of as yet uncatalogued material. The GMB Collection – material donated by the GMB general union from the archives of its predecessor organizations, including the boilermakers' union, the tailors' and garment workers' union, and the white collar union Apex – are a particular strength.

Labour History Archive and Study Centre

103 Princess Street, Manchester M1 6DD
Tel: 0161 228 7212
Web: http://www.phm.org.uk
The Labour History Archive and Study Centre is the main specialist repository for research into the political wing of the labour movement. It holds archives of working-class organizations from the Chartists onwards, including the official archives of the Labour Party and the Communist Party of Great Britain. Other archives include those of the Socialist Sunday Schools movement and the left-wing Unity Trust Theatre. NB: the archive and study centre will be closed to researchers during mid to late 2009 to enable the collections to be moved to the new People's History Museum.

People's History Museum

103 Princess Street, Manchester M1 6DD
Tel: 0161 228 7212
Web: http://www.phm.org.uk
The Manchester-based People's History Museum incorporates both the former National Museum of Labour History and the Pump House People's History Museum. The museum is undergoing an extensive revamp and plans to reopen in late 2009, when it will once again be possible to see some of its collection of trade union banners and other labour movement artefacts dating from Peterloo onwards. The museum houses the TUC's own collection of 6,000 union badges and is the UK's leading authority on the conservation and study of banners. There are more than 400 banners in the collection including the world's oldest trade union banner, that of the Liverpool Tinplate Workers of 1821.

TUC Library Collections

Holloway Road Learning Centre, 236–250 Holloway Road, London N7 6PP
Tel: 020 7133 2260
Web: http://www.londonmet.ac.uk/services/sas/library-services/tuc

Housed at London Metropolitan University, the TUC Library Collections include what is probably the most extensive collection of UK trade union journals and pamphlets in existence. The TUC Library was established in 1922 and was based on the integrated collections of the TUC Parliamentary Committee, the Labour Party Information Bureau, and the Women's Trade Union League. It was run as a joint library with the Labour Party until the TUC moved to Congress House in 1956. The Collections moved to their new home in 1996.

A great deal of material held in the collections has been used to create a free website called The Union Makes us Strong (http://www.unionhistory.info). Although this lavishly illustrated site uses a tiny proportion of the collection's resources, it offers a great deal to family historians, including searchable delegate lists produced for every TUC conference since 1868, strike pay lists from the Bryant & May matchgirls' strike of 1888, and material from the general strike.

Bishopsgate Institute

Bishopsgate Library, Bishopsgate Institute, 230 Bishopsgate, London EC2M 4QH
Tel: 020 7392 9270
Web: http://www.bishopsgate.org.uk

Bishopsgate Reference Library, opened in 1895, has built up a number of printed and archive collections, including the personal library and papers of the trade unionist and MP for Bethnal Green, George Howell (1833–1910) and the London Co-operative Society archive, which includes minute books, papers, journals and other publications from the late 1800s to the 1970s. Bishopsgate Library also holds reports and minute books of the Co-operative Women's Guild.

London School of Economics

London School of Economics and Political Science, 10 Portugal Street, London, WC2A 2HD

Tel: 020 7955 7223
Web: http://www.lse.ac.uk/library/archive
Key holdings include the papers of the Independent Labour Party from the 1880s onwards and the Liberal Party after 1912. The LSE is also home to the papers of the trade union historians and social reformers Sidney and Beatrice Webb, along with those of trade unionists, including Walter Citrine and Henry Broadhurst. Papers for the Women's Co-operative Guild are also found here. The LSE publishes a guide to its Labour history collections at http://www.lse.ac.uk/library/archive/leaflets/labour_history.pdf.

National Library of Scotland

George IV Bridge, Edinburgh EH1 1EW
Tel: 0131 623 3700
Web: http://www.nls.uk/catalogues/online/labour/index.html
The NLS holds an important collection of papers relating to trade unions in Scotland, with some very old records including correspondence between the Edinburgh Union Society of Journeymen Bookbinders and its sister societies dating back to the 1820s, and the records of Edinburgh Trades Council since its foundation in 1859.

Chapter 2

FROM ILLEGALITY TO UNEASY ACCEPTANCE (1800–1850)

On a cold night in February 1809, a group of working men in the fast-growing industrial Lancashire town of Bolton agreed to form what they would call a Friendly Iron Moulders Society. These were bad years for the iron industry, and in the wake of a slump in business employers were cutting wages and putting men out of work. But with far-reaching laws in force to ban combinations 'in restraint of trade', the foundrymen had to take great care with their new endeavour.

Their objective, the men claimed, was to pursue the 'ancient and most laudable custom' common among working men of all types to form societies 'for the sole purpose of assisting each other in case of Sickness, Old Age, and other Infirmities, and for the Burial of the Dead'. Their true purpose was to go much further than this. But to state their real aims would have been to court prosecution and imprisonment. So cautious were they that it took until 19 June before a set of rules was drawn up, signed by twenty-three moulders (seven of whom witnessed with a cross) and submitted to a broader meeting before then being taken before Salford magistrates for their approval. With their legal fees of £21 19s. 8d. paid, and a declaration from the magistrates that the rules were within the law, the new society could now go about its business. From 7 August 1809, the Friendly Iron Moulders Society began to hold regular monthly meetings at the 'Sign of the Hand and Banner', a Bolton public house run by James Isherwood, who would also act as treasurer.

Within a year, there were new branches of the society in Butterley, Manchester and Sheffield. They were followed by Burnley and Leeds (1811), Preston, St Helens and even London (1813), and by a total of twenty-nine other towns and cities by the time the legal ban on combinations was repealed in 1824.

The Bolton men were not, of course, the first to band together for protection against powerful employers or to seek better pay and conditions. Rather, they were part of a tide of trade unionism that swept across the industrial landscape of the nineteenth century to establish independent and enduring organizations, many of whose trade union descendants can still be found in operation today.

The Pre-History of Trade Unions

Trade union historians often point to antecedents among the medieval guilds as evidence of the movement's long past. Certainly, men and women have been combining at work for many centuries in search of better pay and conditions. Writing at the end of the nineteenth century, Sidney and Beatrice Webb, the first historians of the trade union movement, cite disputes involving journeymen cordwainers, saddlers and tailors as far back as the fourteenth century.

But there is no real evidence that these 'Bachelor Companies' through which the journeymen and apprentices organized themselves were in any real sense forerunners of today's unions. Where there is any evidence at all that these were more than ephemeral ad hoc groups, it appears that they were merely junior branches of the masters' guilds, with funds allocated and officers appointed by the masters.

The first trade unions as we would now understand them did not emerge until the later years of the eighteenth century, with the growth of large-scale employers and the end for most workers of any prospect that they would one day become a master themselves. At this time trade unionism was also closely intertwined with the newly emerging friendly societies, and usually performed the same social support function for their own members. As in the case of the iron founders, many of the new trade unions certainly saw enormous benefit in being able to meet legally for these important purposes, no matter how much more widely their discussions and activities may have ranged.

Trades Clubs

Skilled journeymen had first begun to form friendly societies and box clubs to safeguard themselves against the financial calamities of sickness, accidents and old age as far back as the seventeenth century. These were almost always very small clubs, operating along democratic lines with a chairman and committee, which met regularly at a local public house (one of the few public meeting places available to working men) to regulate their affairs.

Such clubs were exclusive in their membership. Few would accept members over the age of forty or those in the most noxious trades since such individuals were more likely to draw on the club's limited resources. Some, such as the Bristol Union of Carpenters, formed in 1768, refused admission to those earning less than 10s. 6d. a week – and in any event, the requirement to maintain regular contribution payments effectively excluded the great bulk of workers whose incomes were too low and too erratic to make this a realistic prospect. Given the tight social networks associated with the skilled artisan trades able to maintain these clubs – such as the printers, shipbuilders and tailors – they also tended to become single-trade bodies, mostly associated with a handful of small workplaces. It was among men such as these – skilled artisan journeymen, often working in traditional industries – that benefits clubs became trades societies and laid the foundations of modern trade unions.

In parallel with the benefits club, three other institutions formed the basis of trades organization at the end of the eighteenth century and into the early years of the nineteenth: the decaying though still important apprenticeship system, the tradition of 'tramping', and the 'house of call'. Each of these was crucial to the journeymen's ability to protect their wages and to prevent the dilution of their craft by less skilled workers. By putting pressure on master craftsmen to restrict the number of apprentices they would take on, and seeking to ensure that only 'legal' men – those who had served their full apprenticeship – were given work, journeymen could hope to restrict the supply of labour which maintained wages. At times when work was short, younger journeymen would also be encouraged to go 'on tramp' – travelling the country in search of towns where there was greater demand for labour. These travelling members were supplied with a 'blank', in effect the earliest form of trade union membership card, which proved their credentials to the journeymen clubs of other towns and guaranteed them a meal and bed for the night at the 'house of call' – often the public house at which the club held its regular meetings. Through these means, trades societies were able to establish friendly relationships and effective networks. The era of national trade unions, however, remained some way in the future.

The Era of the Combination Acts

The Combination Acts of 1799 and 1800 did not make unions illegal. There were already laws to prevent workers 'combining' against their employers dating back to at least the early 1300s, and during the eighteenth century alone there were more than forty Acts of Parliament forbidding combinations in various trades. But by making it easier to bring a prosecution before the justices rather than in a jury court, the Combination Acts certainly made it more difficult for working men to organize and act collectively in their own interests, and brought a bitterness to industrial relations that would not be easily forgotten.

In the final years of the eighteenth century, war with France had led to high inflation – and in turn to an unprecedented level of wage demands and industrial unrest. With skilled labour in short supply, few employers were able to hold out against the journeymen, and trades clubs were becoming increasingly organized and effective in presenting their demands. It was against this background and as part of a wider crackdown on radical activity that the Combination Act of 1799 – originally intended as a limited measure aimed at millwrights – entered the statute book. The measure was a tremendous shock to the trades societies, and petitions poured in to Parliament from the trades of London, Manchester, Bristol, Plymouth, Liverpool, Newcastle and elsewhere seeking its repeal. But to little avail.

The new law apparently failed to check the growth of trade unionism. The London tailors, who had established a highly disciplined and effective union in the 1790s, managed to gain pay rises in 1795, and again following the passing of the Combination Acts in 1801, 1807, 1810 and 1813. London's shoemakers, carpenters, brushmakers, compositors, silk weavers and tin-plate workers all managed during these years to establish means of wage bargaining with their masters.

But the law did place trade unionists in a precarious position and there were numerous prosecutions – even if there are few recorded examples of the Combination Acts themselves being used. In 1810, for example, nineteen printworkers on *The Times* were convicted at the Old Bailey for combining to demand a pay rise. They were fined and sent to prison for two years. There would be further prosecutions in 1823 when weavers and spinners at Tyldesley New Mills in Bolton went on strike in pursuit of an increase in their wages. When the weavers' books were seized, the iron founders were discovered to have been among the most generous donors to the cause.

Sadly, little documentation of use to the family historian survives from this era. Printers have always been among the best organized trades, and a London society of compositors existed as early as 1785. Yet the first records date from 1826. The earliest useful records for family historians are the minutes of the London General Trade Society of Compositors for 1827–34, now in the Modern Records Centre at Warwick University. Similarly, while a brushmakers' society was formed as early as 1747, the earliest union records are those of the London Journeymen Brushmakers, whose minute books dating back to the 1820s are in the Working Class Movement Library in Manchester.

Repeal and Uneasy Legality

The dating of the earliest surviving trade union records to the second half of the 1820s is significant. In 1824, thanks to a brilliant lobbying campaign led by the leading London radical Francis Place which caught almost everyone by surprise, the Combination Acts were repealed, and trade union activity ceased to be a criminal offence. What followed was – almost inevitably – a year of trade union activity and strikes on a previously unseen scale. Big new unions appeared among cotton weavers in Glasgow, Manchester and Bolton. Coopers, bricklayers, sawyers, seamen and silk weavers all formed their own unions. There were strikes by tin-plate workers, cabinetmakers, ladies' shoe makers and rope makers. When carpenters working on the extension of rebuilding of Buckingham Palace went on strike, the Coldstream Guards were called in to restore order.

The excitement did not last. The combination of a sudden slump in trade in the second half of 1825 and new legislation to restore some control over trade union activity the same year once again made life harder for trade unionists.

James Cooper, a founder member in 1834 of the Order of Friendly Boiler Makers' Bolton lodge. Source: *History of the United Society of Boilermakers & Iron & Steel Ship Builders*, by D C Cummings (1905).

Membership certificate issued by the Order of Friendly Boiler Makers to Thomas Mayer, who joined the Bolton lodge in September 1836. Source: *History of the United Society of Boilermakers & Iron & Steel Ship Builders,* by D C Cummings (1905).

And even though they were no longer regarded as criminal conspiracies, unions were viewed with intense suspicion. John White, a founder of the Journeymen Steam Engine and Machine Makers' Friendly Society in 1826, later recalled that he was constantly harassed by the police. As treasurer, he sometimes had as much as £16,000 hidden in the chimney or cellar of his house as the union did not dare to keep its funds in a bank.

Throughout the 1830s and into the 1840s, unions occupied an ambiguous legal position. With the continuing persecution and need to impress on new members the seriousness of their commitment in joining, secret passwords and bloodcurdling initiation rites flourished. When the Huddersfield Branch of the steam engine makers' society was formed in 1831, its first purchases were curtains to keep prying eyes from seeing into the clubhouse, a Bible on which members could swear the oath, and a pistol to ensure the oath was kept. It was hardly alone in this.

Among the ceremonial wear acquired by the Preston joiners when their society affiliated to the Operative Builders' Union in 1833 were a topcoat, 'coct hat' and false moustache for the tyler or doorkeeper, while the Warrington society invested 2s. 6d. in painting and gilding the axe used in its admission ceremonies. The sums involved could be substantial. In 1833, the Warrington masons spent £5 2s. on regalia, out of a total income for the previous two years of just £17 4s.

Later in the century, trade unionists would look back on such activity as somewhat embarrassing, but when unions lacked even basic legal protection for their funds against dishonest officials and members could face imprisonment for their trade union activities, bloodthirsty oaths and fearful ceremonies were often the only means they had to try to instil in new recruits the seriousness of their commitments to the union and their comrades.

JOINING THE OPERATIVE BUILDERS' UNION, 1834

Lodge members would first sing a verse to the tune of a familiar hymn and join in prayer before the President declared the meeting open. The Inside Tyler (doorkeeper) then formally asked a question of the First Conductor and reported to the President that the Conductor was outside with strangers desiring admittance. The strangers were admitted, and after a few words from the 'brother' on the left side of the Vice-President, and the singing of another short hymn, they were told to kneel and read the ninetieth psalm. They were now formally certified as masons by the Warden, and the President addressed them in a long doggerel poem.

Pointing to a skeleton, the President would intone:

Strangers, mark well this shadow which now you see,
'Tis a faithful emblem of man's destiny.
Behold this head, once fill'd with pregnant wit;
These hollow holes once sparkling eyes did fit;
This empty mouth no tongue or lips contains;
Of a once well-furnished head see all that now remains;
Behold this breast where a generous heart once moved
Filled with affection loving, and behold –
Mark well these bones: the flesh hath left its place,
These arms could once a tender wife embrace,
These legs in gay activity could roam.
But alas, the spirit fled and all is gone.

O Death, O Death, thy terror strikes us with dismay,
'Tis only the just spirit, that hath left its early clay,
Can set thee at defiance, and in triumph say:
O Death where is thy sting, O grave where is thy victory?
The sting of death is sin, and we are sinners all:
The heavy strike of death must one day on us fall.

Having put the fear of death into the candidates for membership, the Vice-President then asked some questions about their resolution to keep all the secrets of the union. These being answered satisfactorily, each candidate then swore, with one hand on his naked breast and the other on the Bible, to remain loyal to the society and swore, on his life, to keep all its affairs and ritual secret.

Each step in the ceremony was punctuated by the singing of the same short hymn. At its end, with the candidates now properly initiated, the lodge closed with the singing of another specially written verse. It was an experience they could hardly forget.

Adapted from *The Builders' History*, by Raymond Postgate (National Federation of Building Trade Operatives, 1923).

General Unions and Unity

Although the first attempt to form a co-ordinating body for trade union activities had taken place as early as 1818 when the body known as the Philanthropic Hercules briefly brought together activists from as many as thirty or forty London trade societies, there was little real prospect of success while the Combination Acts remained in place. In fact, it was the campaign against moves to reintroduce repressive anti-union legislation during 1824 and 1825 which gave the initiative an early boost, bringing together a London trades committee, the Manchester Artizans' General Committee and similar bodies in Birmingham, Sheffield and Sunderland.

It was the same recognition of the need for unity and co-operation that also led to the launch of *The Trades Newspaper* in 1825. Owned and funded by the London trades societies, the paper carried regular news on wages and combinations, reports on the activities of the societies which owned it, and news of union activities in the provinces. Despite the best efforts of London trade union leaders, including John Gast of the shipwrights (see box), the paper failed to establish a general readership and its distribution outside the capital was at best spasmodic.

Outside London, some of the most important areas of trade union activity in the late 1820s were around the cotton towns of Lancashire. There was a long tradition of spinners' societies being formed in Preston, Manchester, Oldham and elsewhere dating back to the 1790s, but after the repeal of the Combination Acts and the failure of a six-month strike by Manchester spinners, John Doherty, the Irish-born leader of the Manchester Spinners' Society convened a meeting which led to the creation of a Grand General Union of Operative Spinners of the United Kingdom. This was followed a few weeks later by the setting up of a Manchester-based General Union of Trades, which for a time attracted around 150 separate unions into membership, and the launch of the *United Trades' Co-operative Journal*.

Though neither the General Union nor the newspaper lasted long, the scene was now set for the emergence of the most significant move in the direction of general trade unionism, the Grand National Consolidated Trades Union.

UNION LIVES: JOHN GAST (1772–1837)

John Gast was among the best-known trade unionists of his time – condemned by *The Times* as 'the destroyer of the Thames shipping trade', and closely linked both to the would-be revolutionaries behind the Cato Street conspiracy and to the founders of Chartism.

Born in Bristol in 1772, Gast was apprenticed at the age of 16 to one of the largest shipbuilders in the city. He became a journeyman in 1793 and as a time-served apprentice was able to join the society of shipwrights at Bristol. But the following year saw a shipwrights' strike in the city and Gast left soon afterwards – later blaming the 'overbearing and despotic masters' who controlled the industry locally. He arrived at Portsmouth naval dockyard in January 1797, where he swiftly managed to impress his fellow shipwrights and was elected to lead negotiations on their behalf. Soon afterwards, he was once more forced to move on, when the dockyard reduced its labour force by dismissing all those taken on in the previous twelve months.

Moving to London, Gast found work at John Dudman's – one of the biggest shipbuilding yards in the country, where he would remain until 1814. Gast appears to have settled in Deptford: he became a dissenting preacher, by 1802 was regarded as the leader of the Thames shipwrights, and in 1810 took over the 'King of Prussia' public house in Union Street (now renamed Albury Street).

Gast was renowned as an outstanding public speaker and took on numerous roles on behalf of the shipwrights. In 1811, he would be at the forefront of a failed attempt to organize a shipwrights' trade union, and of a rather more successful initiative to found the Hearts of Oak Society to build almshouses for aged shipwrights. Under his leadership, the Thames shipwrights were also prominent in an apprenticeship campaign which saw trade societies attempt to bring prosecutions against masters employing unqualified men.

When peace came to Europe in 1814, shipbuilding was devastated. Gast became president of the new Philanthropic Hercules. Thrown out of work once again by the failure of his employer's business, Gast turned to ultra-radical London politics. He gravitated towards the Spenceans, a revolutionary group some of whose members favoured the assassination of government ministers as a means of advancing the cause of democracy. In the confusion that followed the Peterloo massacre in 1819, Gast appears to have gone along with plans for a violent overthrow of the government, and was suggested as a possible minister in the regime which would follow. Aware of the conspiracy, police stormed a meeting of the conspirators in Cato Street, and in the melee, one policeman was killed. Five men were found guilty of high treason and executed. It was Gast's good luck that he was not present on the night.

With the repeal of the Combination Acts, Gast became secretary of the new Thames Shipwrights' Provident Union. The new union spread rapidly through London's shipyards and soon had nearly 1,400 members. With a powerful network of local committee-men able to negotiate with autonomy inside the yards, it proved itself capable of winning disputes with such regularity that the shipyard owners were among the most prominent advocates of a return to the Combination Acts.

Gast would continue his active involvement in London radical politics for a further decade. He was a leading figure in the National Union of the Working Classes, formed in 1831, which campaigned for universal suffrage and annual elections, but was prepared to see the Reform Act of 1832 as a step in the right direction. He would also play a part in the campaigns of the 1830s against newspaper stamp duty – the 'taxes on knowledge', and in 1836 was a founder member of the London Working Men's Association. Gast died in 1837, just as the LWMA was giving birth to the Chartist movement.

The Grand National and the Tolpuddle Martyrs

The growth of larger regional and even national trade union bodies at the beginning of the 1830s coincided with a growing interest among union activists in co-operative ideals, and attracted the interest of Robert Owen, whose utopian factory communities had made him a highly influential figure in the co-operative movement. Towards the end of 1833, Owen outlined proposals for both a national union representing all trades and for the formation of 'National Companies' which would eventually take control of manufacturing.

Practical steps to turn the plan into reality took place at a conference in London in February 1834 at which it was agreed that the new body – to be called the Grand National Consolidated Trades Union – would take the form of a federation of separate trade lodges, each made up of the members of one trade. Each lodge would hold its own funds, but there would be levies to support strikes. The conference also adopted a common initiation rite and solemn oath.

Memorial to the Tolpuddle Martyrs in the Dorset village today. Photo: Mark Crail.

Within a few weeks the new union had recruited at least half a million members, both by signing up existing union lodges and by establishing new ones. Among those adhering to the union were the Belfast cabinetmakers, the Perthshire ploughmen, and the 'agricultural and other labourers' of Kensington, Fulham and Hammersmith. Women were also permitted to join, with the Grand Lodge of Operative Bonnet Makers and the Lodge of Female Tailors among those affiliating to the GNCTU.

The weaknesses of the new organization quickly became apparent. The Leicester hosiers' decision to affiliate to the union led to a disastrous dispute in which more than 1,300 men had to be supported, and in Glasgow a further 1,500 men, women and children were locked out for refusing to abandon the union. Despite a levy of one shilling a head, the GNCTU's efforts to support the 'Derby turn-outs' proved inadequate and they were forced back to work after four months. The union lost further public sympathy when London gas stokers were discovered to be planning a strike which would leave the capital in darkness. They were dismissed and replaced with non-union men.

The most crushing blow, however, came in the village of Tolpuddle. When their already low wages were cut from nine to seven shillings, and with the threat of a further cut ahead, a small group of agricultural labourers agreed on their plan of action. As George Loveless, a Methodist preacher and the leader of the group, later recalled:

> It was resolved to form a friendly society among the labourers, having sufficiently learned that it would be vain to seek redress either of employers, magistrates, or parsons. I inquired of a brother to get information how to proceed, and shortly after, two delegates from a Trade Society paid us a visit, formed a Friendly Society among the labourers, and gave us directions how to proceed.

The 'trade society' was, of course, the Grand National Consolidated Trades Union, and it was to be the initiation rite agreed at the union's founding conference that proved to be its downfall. Soon after the Dorset labourers met for the first time, six of their number were arrested and put on trial at Dorchester Crown Court, accused of administering illegal oaths under the Mutiny Act. In March 1834, they were found guilty and sentenced to be transported to Australia for seven years.

The sentence and its execution sparked an enormous outcry, with tens of thousands marching through London to demand a pardon and extensive lobbying by Radical MPs within Parliament. The setting up of a London Dorchester Committee of prominent trade union members ensured that funds were raised and the pressure to release the 'Tolpuddle martyrs' maintained. But by the time the campaign eventually succeeded and pardons were granted in 1836, the GNCTU had already disappeared. Lockouts and strikes involving London building workers, Leeds clothiers, Oldham cotton spinners and others during the summer of 1834 utterly exhausted the GNCTU's ability to provide financial support, and – not for the last time – employers were able to demand a written renunciation of trade union membership as the price of a return to work.

Towards Chartism

With national organization now in tatters, trade union membership went into decline in the latter half of the 1830s as conditions of trade worsened. Even the strongest of the surviving unions, the Operative Stone Masons, was reduced to near bankruptcy by an ill-advised strike involving masons working on the rebuilding of the Houses of Parliament and the construction of Nelson's Column. Other unions were crippled by the heavy demands on their funds made by unemployed members.

The most significant movement to arise from these desperate times, however, would never enjoy anything more than an uneasy relationship with trade unions. Chartism certainly drew its supporters from much the same milieu as the unions: the London Working Men's Association, which originated the People's Charter, was a continuation of the radical artisan movement in the capital, while the great mass of supporters drawn to Chartism across much of the North of England and in the central belt of Scotland were the industrial workers who had made the spinners' and weavers' unions powerful in more prosperous times. It is also true that many prominent Chartists both at local and national levels were also well-known trade unionists. But with union leaders cautious of any involvement with political causes, and leading Chartists equally cautious of anything which might divert energy from their objectives, the organizational links remained at best loose.

During the summer of 1842, however, the two causes came together in a most spectacular way. In the wake of a round of wage cuts, a series of strikes broke out in the collieries of Staffordshire and the cotton mills of Lancashire and Cheshire. As the strike wave grew and spread as far north as Scotland and down into South Wales, mass meetings were held and huge groups of factory workers walked from town to town to 'turn out' those still working. By accident or design, in August 1842 the main Chartist organization was holding a delegate conference in Ashton-under-Lyne at which all its principal national leaders were present. With striking workers now setting up 'committees of public safety' to decide which factories should continue to operate, and even for a time taking control of the centre of Manchester from the authorities, the Chartist conference came under pressure to put itself and its demands at the head of the strike movement. Reluctantly, fearing that it was being set up, the conference finally did so, and the demand for the Charter became a prominent part of the strikers' rhetoric. As the authorities regained control at the point of fixed bayonets, and with many of the strike's leading figures under arrest, the strike rapidly came to an end. In its aftermath, the strike was largely presented as an episode of mob violence and criminality – and dubbed the 'plug plot', after the practice of stopping factory boilers by removing the plug. With hindsight, it was the first general strike to hit Britain.

As Chartism developed over the years and became a more consciously working-class movement, its leaders worked hard to establish good working links with trade unionists. In 1845, Chartists were prominent in the National Conference of Trades which for a time succeeded in establishing an umbrella body for many smaller unions but failed to attract the bigger union organizations. But as the decade ended and the economic picture brightened, Chartism ceased to be a mass organization and the unions returned to their usual preoccupations of wages, terms and conditions.

Union Papers from the Period

The Working Class Movement Library in Salford has sets of *The Trades Newspaper and Mechanics' Weekly Journal* from 17 July 1825 to 27 December 1828. It also holds records of early brushmakers' trade unions, including minute books of the Society of Journeymen Brush-Makers dating back to 1829 and a list of journeymen brushmakers and apprentices for the same year. Full details of the archive can be found at http://www.wcml.org.uk/holdings/brushmakers.htm.

The Steam Engine Makers' Society was founded in 1824 and has left detailed records. Some very early papers can be found in the **Bishopsgate Institute**. These are listed here: http://www.geog.port. ac.uk/lifeline/sem_db/sem_records.html.

The Francis Place Papers at the **British Museum** are an important source for any study of London radicalism in the early nineteenth century. A selection of these can be found on the British History Online website at http://www.british-history.ac.uk/source.aspx? pubid=230.

Tyldesley and District Historical Society has an account of the Tyldesley weavers' strike of 1823 on its website at http://www.arnw 02593.pwp.blueyonder.co.uk/strike.htm.

The Tolpuddle Martyrs Museum in Tolpuddle is open to the public. Further information about the museum and its opening times can be found at http://www.tolpuddlemartyrs.org.uk. An annual march and music festival to commemorate the martyrs takes place in Tolpuddle every July. Further information can be found on the TUC website at http://www.tuc.org.uk/the_tuc/index.cfm?mins=75& minors=75.

Further Reading

Iorwerth Prothero's *Artisans and Politics in Nineteenth-Century London: John Gast and his Times* (Wm Dawson & Son, 1979) is an excellent source on the numerous organizational twists and turns of trade unions and radical political organization in the capital.

Raymond Postgate's *The Builders History* (National Federation of Building Trade Operatives, 1923) provides a detailed account of early trade union organization in the different building trades.

Chapter 3

FROM NEW MODEL UNIONS TO THE NEW UNIONISM (1851–1900)

With the formation of the Amalgamated Society of Engineers in 1851, a new force emerged in trade unionism which would reshape the labour movement. Created through the amalgamation of a number of smaller engineering unions, the ASE (or Amalgamated Society of Engineers, Machinists, Millwrights, Smiths and Pattern Makers, to give the union its full name) could within a matter of months claim a membership of 11,000 – more than double that of the next largest unions – and an annual income of £500 a week. The ASE's size and wealth alone would have made it a significant body, but it was the adoption of a 'New Model' of organization that would transform trade unionism.

Under the guidance of William Allan, a railway engineer and general secretary of the Journeymen Steam Engine and Machine Makers' Society who took on the leadership of the new union, extensive power was centralized in a national executive and at the union's head office in London. Union branches, which had traditionally been almost completely independent of central control, now administered benefit funds in accordance with strict rules, and could dispense strike pay only with the authorization of the centre. The new society also abandoned the tradition of secrecy that had hung over trade unions in the era of illegality, and almost all circulars and reports were published.

Almost immediately, the ASE was plunged into a struggle with engineering employers which would have destroyed many lesser organizations. In April 1851, engineers at the Oldham firm of Hibbert and Platt had successfully demanded the end of systematic overtime and piecework. Following a vote by the ASE's entire membership, the society put similar demands to other employers. Their response, on

1 January 1851, was to lock out 3,500 engineers and nearly 10,000 labourers until such time as they signed a document pledging that they would neither join nor support any trade union.

Over three months, the ASE paid out £35,792 in benefits to its members and a further £7,767 to non-members who had also been locked out. Eventually, however, with the society's funds exhausted and unable to borrow enough money to keep the fight going, the ASE executive authorized a return to work and agreed that members who signed 'the Document' under duress would not be excluded from membership. It was a heavy defeat, but one from which the ASE made a swift recovery, building both its membership and funds to create a powerful and wealthy union.

Within a few years of the creation of the ASE, this New Model of trade union organization – centralized, disciplined, and reliant on a cadre of full-time officials who saw themselves as organizers rather than as agitators – had been adopted by other unions. The Amalgamated Society of Carpenters and Joiners, founded in 1860 through the merger of a number of small London-based clubs, was initially just 1,000 strong. Under its second general secretary, Robert Applegarth, who took over in 1862, membership grew to 10,000 in the space of just eight years.

The emergence of these New Model unions is as significant for family historians as it is for trade union historians, as their centralized structures required the creation and maintenance of proper records and the new full-time officials were generally just the sort of people to excel at such administrative tasks. As a result, the volume of surviving records is far more substantial from this era onwards, and the chances of being able to identify individual members and activists is all the greater.

Moderation and Legal Recognition

With unions increasingly becoming centralized, national organizations with head offices near to the centres of power in London, it was natural that their full-time officials would come into close and regular contact. During the 1860s, a cluster of like-minded officials grew up around Allan of the ASE and Applegarth of the ASC&J. These included Daniel Guile, general secretary of the ironfounders, Edwin Coulson of the bricklayers, and George Odger, who though leader of a small union of shoemakers was also an important figure in London radicalism. With its shared caution in matters of industrial relations and commitment to

Robert Applegarth, influential general secretary of the Amalgamated Society of Carpenters and Joiners.
Source: *The Beehive*, June 1873.

lobbying for political reform, this group – known as the Junta – became a dominant force in trade unionism. In time it also attracted support from outside London, including George Howell and Henry Broadhurst from the younger generation of building trade union leaders, the miners' leader Alexander Macdonald and Alexander Campbell, a prominent figure among Glasgow trade unionists. Both Howell and Broadhurst would go on to prominence in the trade union movement before serving as Liberal Members of Parliament.

A significant development dating from the 1850s onwards was the development of trades councils, which sought to provide a forum and centre of organization for trade unions at a local level. Among the first were in Edinburgh (1853), Glasgow (1858), Sheffield (1858) Liverpool (1860) and London (1861). These were to prove particularly important in Scotland, where trade union membership throughout the nineteenth century was lower than in England and the focus of most industrial disputes was local rather than national. However, it was through the London Trades Council that the Junta exercised its influence. With Howell as its secretary, by 1864 the engineers and carpenters provided half its income, and as the trade union historians Sidney and Beatrice Webb noted: 'In the meetings at the old Bell Inn, under the shadow of Newgate, we have the beginnings of an informal Cabinet of the Trade Union world.'

Out of these local trades councils also emerged the most important new trade union organization of the nineteenth and twentieth centuries: the Trades Union Congress or TUC. There had been numerous attempts to form a central, co-ordinating body for trade union activities at a national level – including the short-lived United Kingdom Alliance of Organized Trades in 1866. But it was on the initiative of Manchester and Salford Trades Council (also formed in 1866) that the first meeting of the Trades Union Congress was held in the Mechanics' Institute in Manchester from 2 to 6 June 1868. Just thirty-four delegates, representing some 118,000 trade union members, attended this first Congress. London Trades Council and the Junta initially stood aloof. However, by the end of the century, the TUC was the undisputed national voice of trade unionism.

With trade union illegality now apparently a thing of the past, the unions began to be able to focus their political lobbying on securing their own position and improving the lot of their members. From 1855 unions were able to register as friendly societies, protecting at least their social benefit funds. In 1859 the Combinations of Workmen Act legalized peaceful picketing in pursuit of disputes over pay and working hours. Finally, in 1867 the Master and Servant Act, which it made it a criminal offence for an employee to leave work unfinished – in other words, to go on strike – was made less severe. This was no minor matter: figures obtained by Glasgow Trades Council showed there to be more than 10,000 such cases coming before the courts each year.

Two developments in 1867, however, threatened to set back all the progress made to date. A series of violent attacks by trade unionists on non-union members in Sheffield culminated in the blowing up of a workman's house, provoking the setting up of a royal commission on trade unions. More prosaically but no less seriously, when the treasurer of the Bradford branch of the boilermakers' society stole £24 from union funds, the courts ruled that union funds were not protected by law and could not be recovered. The decision was upheld on appeal, where it was also held that though trade unions had ceased to be criminal organizations, they remained illegal associations because they acted in 'restraint of trade'. The implication was that their funds could be embezzled with impunity.

Applegarth of the Association of Carpenters and Joiners worked ceaselessly in briefing friendly members of the royal commission and himself gave evidence before it. Although the majority report proved hostile, a minority report signed by four members recommended the repeal of legislation preventing unions from carrying out their jobs and giving full protection for union funds. With the election of a new Liberal government under William Gladstone, these measures now became law in the Trade Union Act of 1871.

The cautious leadership of the Junta and its emphasis on legal reform were not universally popular, however, and throughout the 1860s opposition centred around *The Beehive*, a newspaper established by George Potter, the leader of a small London carpenters' union. An 1864 strike by the General Union of Operative Carpenters was condemned by the London Trades Council under Applegarth's influence, alienating many building trade workers. The Junta was also highly critical of other groups of trade unionists it thought unreasonable. Nor did their approach guarantee industrial harmony, and employers increasingly turned to the use of the lockout to enforce their will. Staffordshire ironworkers, Clyde shipbuilders and South Yorkshire miners all fell foul of the tactic.

The Benefits of Membership

The well-run New Model unions of this era were generous in supporting their own members in hard times, and this required sound financial management. The Amalgamated Society of Carpenters and Joiners on its formation in 1860 was prepared to bring existing unions into the amalgamation only if they could prove that their reserves averaged at least 10 shillings a member. Members of these existing societies could then join the ASC&J on payment of 5 shillings entrance fee and 3d. a week contributions.

As a result, the union was able to offer its members up to £15 compensation in the event of a potentially catastrophic loss of their workman's tools, and in addition to the usual sickness and unemployment benefits, a funeral benefit of £7 in the event of the member's death and £3 in the event that his wife should die. When funds were sufficient, the union was also prepared to pay unemployed members with five years' standing a grant of £6 to help them begin a new life in the colonies. Payments of this sort remained in the union's rule book until as late as 1892.

SECRETARIES' ADDRESSES.

1. *Lambeth.*—Thomas Selby, 7 Warwick-place-west, Warwick-street, Pimlico, London.
2. *Borough.*—Henry Clayden, 35 Great Suffolk-street, Borough, London.
3. *King's Cross.*—John Snow, 5 Smith-street, King's Cross, London.
4. *Drury Lane.*—E. W. Ward, 7 East Harding-street, Gough-square, Fleet-street, London.
5. *Stepney.*—Josh. Wilkinson, 16 Old Norfolk-street, Stepney, London.
6. *Paddington.*—John Salmon, 23 Hardington-street, Portman-market. London.
7. *Pimlico.*—William Harry, 7 Richard's-place, First-street, Marlborough-road, Chelsea, London.
8. *Camberwell.*—William Edward Cracknell, 11 Clarendon-place, Camberwell-new-road, London.
9. *Camden Town.*—Joseph Pollard, 151 Great College-street, Camden-town, London.
10. *Portman Square.*—George Green, 5 John-street-north, Marylebone-road, London.
11. *Edgware Road.*—George Shepherd, 18 Dorset-buildings, Upper Park-place, Dorset-square, London, N.W.
12. *Norwood.*—Charles Wilson, 2 Chapel-place, Chapel-road, Lower Norwood, London.
13. *Notting Hill.*—Edward Hingston, 8 St. Ann's-road, Royal-crescent, Notting Hill, London.
14. *Pimlico 2nd.*—M. W. Meade, 17 Alfred-road, Battersea-park, London.
15. *Chelsea.*—Thomas Jones, 26 Blenheim-street, Chelsea, London.
16. *Manchester Square.*—Edmund Pope, 48, Star-street, Edgware-road, London.
17. *Kidderminster.*—Charles Croft, Park-lane-terrace, Kidderminster.
18. *Richmond.*—Charles Loveday, 2 Red Lion-street, Richmond, Surrey (London district).
19. *Devonport.*—James Babb, 27 Garden-street, Morice-town, Devonport, Devon.
20. *Bloomsbury.*—Joseph Barry, 5 Smart's-buildings, High Holborn, London.
21. *Gray's Inn Road.*—George West, 21 Harrison-street, Gray's Inn-road, London.

Branch secretaries of the Amalgamated Society of Carpenters and Joiners, recorded in the union's first annual report in December 1860. Source: author's collection.

The ASC&J also made provision for those who worked for it. Branch secretaries would receive 6s. 3d. a quarter for a branch of ten members and £1 6s. 3d. for 100. However, in keeping with the unions' new-found respectability, the rules stated that: 'He must not keep a beerhouse.' The general secretary, a full-time post, was paid 33s. a week and 7s. 6d. for office assistance, with an extra allowance of 2s. for each council meeting. Had the general secretary continued to work at his trade he could have expected to earn something very similar.

Well run and financially astute as they were, however, the New Model unions did not see it as their role to organize or fight for less skilled workers. Rather, a main focus of their activity was centred on keeping wages high by reducing and controlling the supply of labour – insisting that no journeyman should have more than one apprentice, and that only those who completed their apprenticeship should be allowed to carry out skilled work.

Unions and the Liberal Party

The trade union leadership of the 1870s was overwhelmingly cautious in its industrial policy and focused instead on influencing Whitehall and Westminster by lobbying MPs and ministers, and giving expert evidence on issues affecting working men. So standing trade union-backed candidates in parliamentary elections came as a logical next step.

Within a few years, the combination of union leadership and Liberalism would come to be the norm. The first tentative steps in parliamentary politics, however, were provoked by dissatisfaction with the Liberal government's failure to support a Nine Hours Bill limiting the working day. In 1869 and 1870 a Labour Representation League composed of prominent trade unionists ran George Odger as an independent Labour candidate, and in 1874, backed for the first time with union money, thirteen 'Labour' candidates went to the poll. Accepting what would otherwise have been the inevitable loss of their seats at Stafford and Morpeth, the Liberals stood down, allowing Alexander Macdonald and Thomas Burt of the miners' union to become the first 'Labour members' of the House of Commons.

From this date, the Labour Representation League and the Liberal Party worked together to support the election of working men to Parliament as 'Lib-Lab' MPs. One of the first to be elected in this way was Henry Broadhurst of the Operative Society of Stonemasons, who both served on the TUC's parliamentary committee and was secretary to the Labour Representation League. With Liberal backing, Broadhurst became MP for Stoke in 1880, and subsequently represented the Bordesley seat in Birmingham from 1885. In the same year, Lib-Lab politics reached a high point, with twelve working men elected.

Unfortunately, Broadhurst's subsequent parliamentary career reflected growing tensions between the Liberal Party and trade unionists which would eventually lead to the emergence of the Labour Party. Offered a junior minister's job at the Home Office, Broadhurst soon found himself arguing against the introduction of an eight-hour day. Broadhurst's own union joined the revolt against him when in 1890 the TUC reaffirmed its support for just such legislation, and in 1892 he lost his seat in Parliament when working men refused to back him. Although Broadhurst returned to Parliament two years later and remained an MP until 1906, he had cut his ties with the trade union movement.

UNION LIVES: WILLIAM DAVIS (1848–1934)

William Davis epitomized a generation of trade union leaders who, during the 1870s and 1880s, turned the unions into a respectable pillar of the Liberal establishment.

The son of a brassfounder, Davis followed his father into the trade, becoming a chandelier maker and assembler. He also became involved in politics, and in 1869 represented the Birmingham Barr Street Reform Association at the second Trades Union Congress. When, in 1871, a pay dispute led to the creation of the Amalgamated Society of Brassworkers, Davis was chosen as general secretary. With a five-year break during which he served as a factory inspector, he would remain in post until 1921.

Davis proved effective at building union membership, and his firm but conciliatory attitude towards industrial relations proved highly effective. Like many of his generation, Davis opposed the employment of women in skilled trades – and even organized a strike at one factory in support of his cause. He would continue to clash with women trade unionists at TUC conferences from the 1870s through to the end of the Edwardian era.

Davis was an active proponent of Lib-Lab politics, seeking independent representation for working men within a Liberal political framework, and served on Birmingham Town Council. A staunch opponent of socialist views, as late as 1918 he backed short-lived moves to create a union-based political party in opposition to the Labour Party.

Davis's support for Britain's role in the Boer War and later the First World War alienated many trade unionists. However, he retained their respect, not least for the active role he took from the 1880s onwards in support of old age pensions, and he counted many leading Labour politicians among his friends, including Ramsay MacDonald and George Lansbury.

Davis retired to live in France with his daughter Mabel, and died there at the age of 86.

New Unionism

If the trade union movement had grown staid and even complacent, the events of 1888 and 1889 were to shake it to its roots and provide a much-needed infusion of new blood.

There had been earlier attempts to organize unskilled workers. Joseph Arch's National Agricultural Labourers' Union, formed in 1872, had rapidly recruited thousands of members in the countryside before the combination of poor harvests and a concerted lockout by employers forced a return to work and led to the union's collapse. Similarly, a Miners' Association of Great Britain, founded in 1842, led a five-month strike before being driven out of existence. Its successor, the Miners' National Union of 1863, was a more moderate body which concentrated on legal and political representation for its members.

However, an article about the plight of matchgirls employed by Bryant & May at its factory in Bow in the East End of London, written by the journalist Annie Besant for *The Link* newspaper, provided a focus both for simmering discontent in the East End and for the new socialist groups now springing up among London's middle-class radicals. Besant had a long record of political activism and, in 1887, had been a principal speaker at a rally of the unemployed in Trafalgar Square. When police tried to break up the assembly, there was fighting in which one man died and hundreds were arrested.

The following year, through a young socialist called Herbert Burroughs, she came into contact with workers at Bryant & May. It was a mostly young and female workforce, poorly paid and subject to terrible industrial diseases, including 'phossy jaw', which caused the girls' bones to rot. After Besant's article appeared under the headline 'White slavery in London', the girls sought her help in setting up a trade union. The resulting strike was to last three weeks and win enormous support among the public and in Parliament. Eventually, with the help of London Trades Council, the newly formed Union of Women Match Makers won all its demands and returned to work.

The effects were twofold. First, the small Women's Trade Union League, led by Clementina Black, Mona Wilson and Gertrude Tuckwell, began to grow in strength as more women flocked to the trade union movement. First set up in 1874, the League had grown only slowly over the previous decade. The Bryant & May strike, however, gave it a much-needed boost. In 1888, Clementina Black was able to move the first successful resolution at a TUC conference calling for

Mona Wilson, secretary to the Women's Trade Union League. Source: TUC Souvenir booklet, 1902.

equal pay, and by the 1890s ten London unions and over thirty provincial unions were affiliated.

The second effect was to give a focus to other groups of unskilled workers suffering the effects of an economic depression. Most famously, the creation of the Dock, Wharf, Riverside and General Labourers' Union in 1889 and the subsequent London dock strike in support of the 'dockers' tanner' – their demand for 6d. an hour for their work – proved to be both successful in its own right and the catalyst for an explosion in trade union membership among unskilled workers.

As John Burns, one of the leading figures in the dock strike, put it:

The labourer has learned that combination can lead him to anything and everything. He has tasted success as the immediate fruit of combination, and he knows that the harvest he has just reaped is not the utmost he can look to gain. Conquering himself, he has learned that he can conquer the world of capital whose generals have been the most ruthless of his oppressors.

The sudden infusion of unskilled workers into the trade union movement effectively spelled the end of the alliance with Liberalism and a turn towards independent labour representation with more than a flavour of socialism. The New Unionism, as it was known, also laid the foundations for two of the twentieth century's biggest unions – the Transport and General Workers' Union and the General and Municipal Workers' Union.

Although the initial excitement did not last, and union membership dropped back considerably by 1900, a fundamental change had taken place and the TUC was no longer the preserve of the relatively well-off and highly skilled labour aristocrats of the craft unions. Over the next few years new unions emerged for transport workers, gas workers, warehousemen, postmen and others who had hitherto defied union organization. Trade unionism also began to win converts among what were called 'black-coated' workers – shop assistants, railway clerks and others in clerical jobs. Their story, however, is mostly a twentieth-century one.

Union Papers from the Period 1851–1900

Amalgamated Society of Engineers

The most extensive collection of papers for the Amalgamated Society of Engineers can be found in the **Modern Records Centre** at **Warwick University**. These include executive council minutes from 1852 to 1917, monthly and annual reports, monthly, quarterly and annual branch financial returns to head office, membership registration books and members' transfer books, along with many district and branch papers. Further information on these holdings can be found at http://www.warwick.ac.uk/services/library/mrc/ead/259ase.htm.

Bishopsgate Institute also has a substantial archive, including seventy-seven volumes of handwritten quarterly branch report forms with notes and figures on income and expenditure, membership numbers, lists of excluded members, quarterly admissions, superannuated members, members who had gone abroad, and the death of members or their wives. Further information about this collection and how to access it can be found at http://www.aim25.ac.uk/cgi-bin/search2?coll_id=7732&inst_id=103.

Amalgamated Society of Carpenters and Joiners

The Modern Records Centre at **Warwick University** holds an incomplete set of union reports from 1860 to 1920, along with some of the union's publications dating back to the late 1860s, executive committee minutes from 1871 onwards and some branch records from the second half of the nineteenth century. It also has membership registers from 1895 to 1921. Various reports produced by the Amalgamated Society of Cabinet Makers, with which the ASC&J merged in 1918, are also at Warwick, as are the mostly later papers of the General Union of Carpenters and Joiners with which it merged in 1921. Further information can be found at http://www2.warwick. ac.uk/services/library/mrc/subject_guides/family_history/carpntr/.

A brief history of the ASC&J including biographies of its full-time officials from 1862 to 1939 can be found on the Trade Union Ancestors website at http://www.unionancestors.co.uk/ASW.htm.

Trades Union Congress

The TUC's official archive is held at the **Modern Records Centre** at **Warwick University**. This includes detailed subject files from 1920 onwards as well as reports, minutes and other papers dating back to its formation in 1868. Further information can be found at http:// www2.warwick.ac.uk/services/library/mrc/archivecatalogues.

The TUC Library Collections, consisting of material built up in the TUC's library over many decades and including a particularly strong collection of trade union publications, is held at **London Metropolitan University**. For further information see http://www.londonmet.ac.uk/ services/sas/library-services/tuc.

The full text of TUC reports where they have survived from 1868 to 1968 can be found on the Union Makes Us Strong website at http://www.tuc.org.uk/the_tuc/index.cfm?mins=72&minors=72. These include the names and addresses of delegates, along with details of their unions, verbatim transcripts of each year's Congress, and other documentation.

A history of the TUC, commissioned for its centenary in 1968, can be found on the TUC website at http://www.tuc.org.uk/the_tuc/index. cfm?mins=72&minors=72.

The archives of the Women's Trade Union League, which became part of the TUC in 1921, are held with the TUC Library Collections at **London Metropolitan University**.

Other archives

A collection of papers collected by **George Howell** during his lifetime as well as a personal archive including letters and diaries is held at **Bishopsgate Institute**.

The **Henry Broadhurst** collection is held at the **London School of Economics**.

The archives of the **Labour Representation League** are held at the **London School of Economics**.

The original strike register showing payments made to participants in the **Bryant & May matchgirls' strike** can be seen on the Union Makes Us Strong website at http://www.unionhistory.info/matchworkers/matchworkers.php.

The personal library and papers of **John Burns** are held in the **London Metropolitan Archives**. The John Burns Collection is in the **Senate House Library** at the **University of London** (http://www.ull.ac.uk/specialcollections/burns.shtml).

Further Reading

There are numerous histories of individual trades councils, many of which are listed on Chelmsford Trades Council's website at http://www.chelmsford-tuc.org.uk/rubrique3.html.

Detailed guides to the legal position of trade unions in the late nineteenth and early twentieth centuries can be found in Douglas Brodie's *A History of British Labour Law, 1867–1945* (Hart Publishing, 2003) and in Mark Curthoys' *Governments, Labour, and the Law in Mid-Victorian Britain: The Trade Union Legislation of the 1870s* (Oxford University Press, 2004).

Growth of selected trade unions, 1855–1900

Union and year founded	1855	1870	1880	1890	1900
Engineers (1851)	12,553	34,711	44,692	67,928	87,672
Carpenters and joiners (1860)	—	10,178	17,764	31,495	65,012
Boilermakers and iron shipbuilders (1832)	—	7,261	17,688	32,926	47,670
Steam engine makers (1824)	1,662	2,819	4,134	5,822	8,566
Iron founders (1809)	5,685	8,994	11,580	14,821	18,357
Bricklayers (1848)	—	1,441	5,700	12,740	38,830
Railway servants (187?)	—	—	8,589	26,360	62,023
Dock labourers (1889)	—	—	—	—	13,388
National Amalgamated Union of Labour (1889)	—	—	—	—	21,111
Postmen (1891)	—	—	—	—	23,180

Sources: for 1855, 1870, 1880, Statistical Tables and Report on Trade Unions, Board of Trade 1888; for 1890, 1900, *The History of Trade Unionism* by Sidney and Beatrice Webb, 1920.

Chapter 4

THE RISE TO POWER
(1901–1945)

Over the first two decades of the twentieth century, the trade union movement grew at a faster rate than at any other time in its history and became markedly more militant. Between 1900 and 1920, the proportion of working men and women in trade unions grew from around one in ten to almost four in ten, while the number of working days lost to industrial disputes each year regularly ran into many millions.

Despite the setbacks of the 1890s, during which many of the new union members brought in during the aftermath of the docks strike melted away, the new century brought with it a period of sustained growth – albeit often from small beginnings. The year 1904 saw the birth of the Association of Shorthand Writers and Typists (later, in 1912,

Members of the Municipal Employees Association Stepney branch committee in their regalia, 1901. Source: author's collection.

to become the Association of Women Clerical Staff) – a small straw in the wind of trade unionism among both women and white collar workers. Two years later, in 1906, the National Federation of Women Workers was created by the amalgamation of some eighty or ninety small unions formed in isolated disputes. Even entertainers joined in, when Marie Lloyd and other leading celebrities of the day led a strike that closed many London music halls for a fortnight in 1907. Five years later, a dispute over pension rights led to the creation of the National Asylum Workers' Union, which would later form much of the basis of health service trade unionism, while in the same year a small, Norfolk-based farmworkers' union became the National Agricultural Labourers' and Rural Workers' Union and laid the foundations for the first enduring union in the countryside since the 1870s.

The Edwardian Era: Legal and Industrial Battles

Throughout this period, though, the trade union movement came under a sustained legal assault which threatened the many gains made

Shop workers protest against the living-in system in 1906.
Source: Union of Shop, Distributive and Allied Workers.

Leaflet advertising a meeting to mark the opening of a new branch of the Amalgamated Society of Railway Servants, 1912.
Source: author's collection.

over the final decades of the nineteenth century. Following a successful strike by members of the Amalgamated Society of Railway Servants for higher wages and union recognition, the Taff Vale Railway Company sued the union for the losses it had incurred. The House of Lords held that the union was responsible for the actions of its members and ordered it to pay compensation of £23,000. This was a devastating ruling, which would have made it impossible for any union to take industrial action without the threat of bankruptcy hanging over it. In the five years that followed, unions faced a series of legal actions from employers, until an incoming Liberal Government brought in the Trade Disputes Act of 1906, which restored unions' immunities once again.

As unions' political sympathies now began to move to the left, a threat to their political activities emerged from within the ranks of Liberal trade unionism. In 1909, Walter V Osborne, the secretary of the Amalgamated Society of Railway Servants' Walthamstow branch and a long-standing Liberal, took the union to court over its use of its political funds to support the new Labour Party. Both the Court of Appeal and the House of Lords held that the union had no right to compel its members to support any political party. This was a particular blow to the Labour Party because the growing number of MPs now being elected in its name generally lacked independent means to support themselves, but it also made it hard for the unions to push through the legal changes they wanted to see to protect their members' interests. The legal battle led to bitter feuding within the trade union movement. The ASRS wound up its Walthamstow branch and expelled Osborne, who in turn became something of a minor political celebrity, writing a book titled *Sane Trade Unionism*. Once again it would take some years for this ruling to be reversed by Parliament, but the Trade Union Act 1913 permitted unions to set up political funds as long as members had the right to opt out of payments to it.

But while these political and legal battles were being fought out in Parliament and the courts, the daily experience of trade unionists was mostly focused on an extraordinary outbreak of militancy that spread over the twenty-four months of 1911 and 1912. This period saw the number of days lost to strikes hit 40 million in a single year – the highest number then on record, and one which has been exceeded only twice more since then. The 'great unrest' as it was dubbed, is often attributed to the growth of syndicalist political ideas among trade unionists disillusioned with party politics. Lacking faith that the new Labour Party would improve their lot and often cynical about their own union leaders, syndicalists believed they could achieve their broadly socialist aims through industrial struggle alone. Influenced by the French socialist leader Daniel de Leon and the Industrial Workers of the World (a radical US-based trade union known as the Wobblies), British and Irish syndicalists including the former docks strike leader Tom Mann and the Irish republican James Connolly proselytized their views in the dockyards, coalfields and industrial centres of the country with great effect.

During 1911, a strike by London printers led to the setting up of the *Daily Herald*, the first pro-Labour newspaper. There were also strikes by railwaymen and transport workers. But for the first time in the twentieth century, 1912 also saw the miners flex their industrial muscle when a national strike by members of the Miners' Federation of Great Britain closed down the coalfields for five weeks from 26 February to 11 April.

UNION LIVES: P C HOFFMANN (1878–1959)

P C Hoffmann's brief career as an MP, from 1923–24 and from 1929–31, was undistinguished. Yet his record as a union organizer deserves more than a footnote in labour history.

Hoffmann had lived the life of a downtrodden shop boy and was instrumental throughout the Edwardian era and beyond in the campaign to abolish compulsory 'living-in' – a system which subjected shopworkers to a petty tyranny that even governed their right to marry.

The son of a wealthy silk mercer, Philip Charles Hoffmann was orphaned at nine and grew up as a boarder at the Warehousemen's, Clerks' and Drapers' School in Purley. He was apprenticed to a Holborn draper at the age of 16.

He would later recall his first experiences of the world of the shop assistant:

> That night I found myself along with half a dozen other young shavers in a small dirty room with six beds packed very close together, covered with coarse red and black counterpanes. The ceiling was very low and could be reached easily by stretching our young arms. Both walls and ceilings were bare, grimy and splotched. The two windows, being curtained with dirt, needed no other obscuring. The naked gas jet had a wire cage over it.
>
> The boys undressed or dressed sitting or standing on their beds – there was so little room otherwise. But there was no bed for me; I had been overlooked. The steward with one eye, who was one of the porters, said I must sleep with one of the others. I refused. I had never done that before. He brought me from somewhere a blanket and a pillow. I lay down with them on the floor between two of those crowded beds. The gas was turned out at the main at 11.15. One of the boys lighted a piece of candle and they hunted for bugs on the wall, cracking them with slipper heels … I sobbed through that dismal night.

Living-in was much disliked. With labour cheap, employers were able to make it a condition of employment, providing poor accommodation and food, charging high prices deducted from wages, and enforcing rules that ranged from compulsory lights-out and church attendance through a system of fines and lockouts. Many were denied the right to vote.

Hoffmann became involved in the shop assistants' union and in June 1901 helped launch a campaign against living-in. After a packed meeting at Westbourne Park Chapel (advertised by Hoffmann and others dressed in top hats and frock coats), the issue became one of the union's central concerns. By 1907, Hoffmann was a full-time union organizer, actively involved in organizing first negotiations and then strikes against the living-in system. First Debenham and Freebody, then D H Evans of Oxford Street and other lesser names in London, Oxford, Newcastle-under-Lyme, and most of all South Wales, caved in and agreed to end living-in.

In Merthyr and Dowlais, however, the campaign faltered. Despite the support of Keir Hardie, two drapers held out, and issued writs for libel against Hoffmann and Hardie's paper, the *Merthyr Pioneer*. Hoffmann was bankrupted by a court order to pay £250. But the campaign went on and by early 1914, the whole of South Wales was free of the living-in system.

Hoffmann became the union's London organizer, leading the fight for union recognition. A strike at the Army and Navy Stores in 1919 laid the groundwork for a London-wide agreement, and a protracted six-week strike at John Lewis of Oxford Street taxed his organizing skills to the full – requiring him at one point to find emergency accommodation for 200 young women who neither would nor could continue to live-in.

In December 1923, Hoffmann stood for Parliament as the Independent Labour Party candidate in South East Essex. He won, but lost the seat the following October and returned to the union as national organizer. Five years later he would again become an MP,

serving from 1929 until Labour's rout after the Ramsay MacDonald split of 1931. His attempt to regain the seat in 1935 failed, and he became union organizer for the Eastern Counties until retirement at age 65.

After retirement, Hoffmann continued to attend conferences of the Union of Shop, Distributive and Allied Workers, which had been formed through amalgamation in 1947. His final conference was at Easter 1959 in Scarborough. Soon afterwards, he died at his home in Hampstead Garden Suburb.

P C Hoffmann. Source: Union of Shop, Distributive and Allied Workers.

Trade Unions and the First World War

The greatest challenge to the trade union movement, however, came with the outbreak of the First World War. There had always been a strong anti-war feeling in the labour movement – in part based on pacifism, and in part influenced by the Marxist political thinking of the Second International, which held that workers had more in common with the workers of another country than with the capitalist class of their own. However, within weeks of the declaration of war the TUC had declared an 'industrial truce' and given its support to the military recruitment campaign. Will Crooks, the veteran leader of the dockers in 1889 and now a Labour MP, now became one of the most enthusiastic advocates of the war, travelling thousands of miles and addressing crowded meetings up and down the land at which he urged young men to join up. He would later be made a Privy Councillor for his efforts.

Opinion in the dockyards and factories over the merits of war would doubtless have been as divided as those at the top of the trade union movement. But there was a sharp divide on the issue of an industrial truce. In 1915, munitions factory workers on Clydeside defied the leadership of the Amalgamated Society of Engineers to go on strike,

Front page of The Railway Clerk, *June 1917. The Railway Clerks' Association benefited from a surge in white collar union membership.*

leading to the creation of a rank-and-file Clyde Workers' Committee chaired by the British Socialist Party (later Communist Party) activist Willie Gallacher. Other industrial centres including Sheffield, Manchester and Birmingham followed the lead set by the 'Red Clydesiders', and while the number of strikes undoubtedly fell during the war, there was never at any time what might be called an 'industrial truce'. For the long term, one of the most important developments to emerge from this divide between union leaders and the shop floor was the shop stewards movement – independent rank-and-file activists who would continue to be an important source of radical local leadership for more than half a century, until unions moved to recognize and incorporate them within their formal structures.

The 1914–18 period also saw a huge influx of women into the workforce. In 1914, 90 per cent of trade union members were men, and 90 per cent of women workers were not trade union members. On the outbreak of war, many women were thrown out of work when middle-class families economized by cutting back on domestic staff. But it soon became apparent that they would be needed in other industries as men left for the Front.

Around 1,600,000 women joined the workforce during the First World War. They worked on public transport, in post offices and government departments, as land workers and in factories. By 1918, munitions factories alone employed 950,000 women workers. But despite the best efforts of women trade union leaders such as Margaret Bondfield and Mary Macarthur to gain union membership rights and equal pay for women war workers, the arrival of a vast number of new workers who were often satisfied with lower rates of pay frequently served to undermine union influence in the workplace. By 1920, the number of women trade unionists had risen to an impressive 1,342,000, but this still represented just one in four of the female workforce.

The 1920s and 1930s: Militancy and Defeat

With the war over, all pretence of peace on the shop floor was swept away. Even the most unlikely groups of workers became involved in strike action, with London barbershops closed over the winter of 1918 when hairdressers downed scissors for seven weeks in pursuit of a pay claim. A massive strike organized by the Clyde Workers' Committee in 1919 was followed by further stoppages in the coal mines and in the transport and print industries. Belfast, too, was paralyzed by a wave of strikes. There were even strikes in the police force which saw tanks brought on to the streets of Liverpool to restore order and Royal Navy battleships rushed back from Scapa Flow. Some 35 million working days were lost that year to industrial disputes. In the wake of the Russian revolution, the fear of a workers' revolt hung heavily over Britain – no more so than during 1926, when a ten-day general strike brought the country to a halt.

The General Strike and its Consequences

In 1925, the British coal industry was in crisis. The richest coal seams had been heavily depleted by the war effort a decade earlier, and productivity was at a low ebb. With Britain now back on the gold standard, making exports expensive, and German producers allowed to re-enter the international coal market, mine owners sought to safeguard their profits by cutting wages and introducing longer working hours. Under pressure from the TUC, however, the Conservative government of Stanley Baldwin intervened to introduce a nine-month subsidy to support miners' wages and set up a royal commission. Although hailed at the time as 'Red Friday' – a victory for the unions – in reality it merely put off the start of a major conflict.

When the commission reported in March 1926, it recommended an end to the miners' subsidy and the restructuring of the industry, but rejected nationalization. The mine owners' response was to demand wage cuts of between 10 and 25 per cent, the introduction of regional pay negotiations and longer working days. They also threatened a lockout if the terms were not accepted by 1 May. On that same day, a conference called by the TUC called a general strike in defence of the miners, to begin on 3 May.

In the days that followed, millions of workers downed tools. Newspapers ceased to publish, trains and buses stopped running and building sites fell silent. In all, an estimated 2.5 million people went on strike on the first day, leaving a further 16 million to find their way to work on foot or bicycle. The government was in many ways better prepared for the conflict than the trade unions, which had to set up committees and structures to deal with communications and to authorize the continued operation of essential services from scratch. All over the country, trades councils transformed themselves into central strike committees or councils of action. Meanwhile, the authorities declared a state of emergency and began to mobilize the armed forces in case the worst should happen. Long queues of middle-class men formed outside the Foreign Office to volunteer their services in opposition to the strike, while at the gentlemen's clubs in Pall Mall and St James's, the upper classes signed up as special constables. For the government, Winston Churchill commandeered the presses of the *Morning Post* and began publication of the *British Gazette* as an anti-strike propaganda tool. The TUC responded with *The British Worker*.

As the strike wore on, the government began to get the upper hand. With army protection, food lorries began to leave the London docks. Some leading members of the TUC became concerned that there would be a drift back to work, while others feared that control of the strike was moving out of the hands of the unions' leaders and coming under the control of more militant local activists. The worst blow came from within the trade union movement, when Havelock Wilson, the maverick leader of the National Sailors' and Firemen's Union, sought a court injunction preventing the TUC from calling his members out on strike without a ballot. The judge, former Liberal MP Sir John Astbury, not only agreed to the injunction, but also declared the strike itself illegal – laying the TUC open to potentially devastating claims for damages.

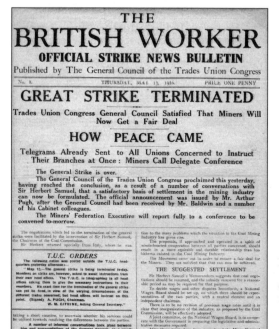

Front page of the TUC's British Worker, *announcing a return to work at the end of the 1926 general strike.* Source: author's collection.

Throughout all this, negotiations both formal and informal had been going on. Exhausted, fearful and uncertain, by 11 May the TUC general council was willing to reach agreement. Although the leaders of the Miners' Federation of Great Britain rejected the proposals outright, members of the general council visited 10 Downing Street the following day to announce that the strike would be called off. They had hoped to receive assurances in return that there would be no victimization of those who had been on strike, but even this was denied them.

By the end of that week, Britain was returning to normal. For some time, however, some train workers held out, seeking promises that there would be no victimization, and the miners themselves fought on for six long months before being starved back to work, their resources exhausted and the union itself split. By the end of November, employers had succeeded in all their aims and more.

Over the course of the year, Britain had lost a record 162 million working days to strike action – a figure which has never been approached since. In the period of anti-union feeling which followed, the government had little difficulty passing the Trade Disputes and Trade Union Act of 1927. The new law forced civil service trade unions to disaffiliate from the TUC, introduced the practice of 'contracting in' rather than 'contracting out' of political funds, clamped down on picketing and outlawed secondary or sympathetic strikes. Trade union membership fell by more than half a million in 1927 alone, and there would never again be a year in which strike days totalled even one-fifth of the number for 1926. Chastened and more than a little scared by their experiences of the nine-day general strike, the leaderships of many unions now moved significantly to the right, pursuing a course of conciliation with employers while simultaneously moving against militants within their ranks by banning known Communists from holding union office.

Reorganizing and Regrouping

Throughout the 1920s and into the 1930s, the trade union movement went through a period of substantial reorganization. In 1921, the TUC created a new General Council to replace the Parliamentary Committee which had previously run its affairs. The General Council had broader powers and was to focus more closely on industrial rather than political and lobbying activities. At the same time, it took over the work of the Women's Trade Union League, and created two reserved seats for women trade unionists.

The most significant development, however, was the emergence of a number of new giant unions and the beginning of a process of rationalization that has drastically reduced the number of unions over the past 100 years (see Appendix 1). Union legislation passed in 1917 had reduced some of the legal barriers to amalgamations and mergers. The first union to take advantage of this was the old Amalgamated Society of Engineers, which in 1920 merged with nine other organizations to form the Amalgamated Engineering Union. It was swiftly followed in 1922 by the Transport and General Workers' Union, based on a number of unions that had emerged from the docks strike thirty years before, and by the National Union of General and Municipal Workers, some of whose component parts could also trace their histories to the New Unionism of the late 1880s.

The creation of the NUGMW also gave a new home to the National Federation of Women Workers. In many instances, however, trade union attitudes to women in the workplace remained decidedly

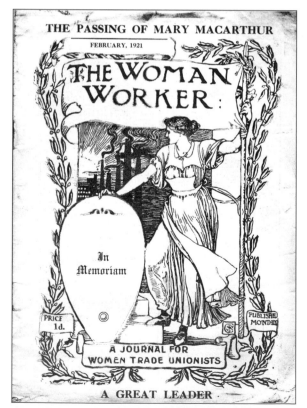

A special issue of The Woman Worker, *published to mark the death of Mary Macarthur, general secretary of the National Federation of Women Workers, 1921.*
Source: author's collection.

hostile, and campaigns for equal pay were quietly forgotten. Although many unions sought to recruit women into membership, they also often sought to restrict the numbers of women able to take jobs in their industries by demanding the introduction or stricter enforcement of rules forbidding married women from employment. In 1935, the Union of Post Office Workers went as far as to issue a straightforward demand for a total block on women's employment. It would take the social upheaval of a Second World War to change such attitudes.

UNION LIVES: MARY MACARTHUR (1880–1921)

As the daughter of a Tory shopkeeper, Mary Macarthur could have gone the way of the young Margaret Roberts (later Mrs Thatcher). Instead, sent by her father to spy on the Ayr branch of the Shop Assistants' Union, she was converted to trade unionism and rapidly became branch secretary.

Through Will Anderson, an activist for the Independent Labour Party and later an MP and chairman of the Labour Party, Macarthur took to socialism. With the support of Margaret Bondfield, later to be the first woman cabinet minister, Macarthur gained the confidence to stand – successfully – for election to her union's national executive.

Moving to London in 1903, she became secretary of the Women's Trade Union League, where she worked closely with James Keir Hardie and Ramsay MacDonald in the campaign to end sweated labour, and established *The Woman Worker* as a monthly magazine. She was also active in the campaign to win the vote for women, opposing moves by the main suffragette organizations to settle for a limited extension of the franchise to middle-class women.

At Macarthur's instigation, the Women's Trade Union League eventually became the women's section of the TUC. During the industrial turbulence of the Edwardian era, she continued to play an active role in leading and supporting strikes by women workers – among them jute workers in Dundee and chainmakers at Cradley Heath in the West Midlands. In 1906, she forged the numerous small unions set up as a result of these disputes into the National Federation of Women Workers, of which she became general secretary.

Macarthur and Anderson married in 1911. An opponent of the First World War, she nonetheless became secretary of the Ministry of Labour's central committee on women's employment. In the 1918 general election, Macarthur stood as the Labour candidate for

Stourbridge but was defeated. The following year, Anderson died in the great flu epidemic.

Macarthur continued to work for the NFWW and helped bring about its merger with two other unions to form the National Union of General and Municipal Workers (today's GMB). Increasingly ill with cancer, however, she did not live to see the outcome of her work. She died on 1 January 1921 – the day the new union came into being.

The Second World War: Into Government

As in 1914, the outbreak of war in 1939 proved difficult for trade unions. There was still a strong pacifist tendency within the labour movement, and the Communist Party of Great Britain remained hostile to the war effort through until 1941, when Hitler's Germany invaded the Soviet Union and the party became the most vociferous supporter of 'the war on fascism'. The efforts of its industrial activists now switched from organizing strikes and denouncing the government to active involvement in the joint production committees set up by the wartime coalition government.

As in 1914, leading trade unionists were brought into government. In May 1940, Ernest Bevin, the general secretary of the Transport and General Workers' Union, was made Minister of Labour and National Service. Bevin adopted a conciliatory approach to trade union demands during the war, but he also came armed with legal powers as draconian as any yet seen. Strikes and lockouts were banned under Order 1305 and the Essential Work (General Provisions) Order of 1941 allowed Bevin to direct skilled workers to wherever they were most needed while also permitting employers to use less skilled workers in previously protected jobs. In 1942, the government would use these legal powers to prosecute more than a thousand miners over a strike at the Betteshanger colliery in Kent. Three union leaders were imprisoned, and many more were fined.

Despite this, the number of strikes continued to rise. In 1943, 12,000 bus workers – many of them members of Bevin's own TGWU – stopped work, as did dockers in Liverpool and Birkenhead. When a total of 3,714,000 days were lost to strikes the following year, the government tightened up the law and with the support of the TUC introduced Defence Regulation 1AA, which outlawed incitement to strike.

Though operating under strict legal controls, the trade union movement managed rapid growth during the Second World War – helped by the government's refusal to award public contracts to companies that failed to comply with union-set minimum standards. Between 1939 and 1945, trade union membership increased from 4.5 million to 7.5 million, and many of these were women – who were once again summoned out of the home and into factories and offices to replace men called up by the armed forces. This time round, even the Amalgamated Engineering Union was forced to reconsider its ban on women workers, and in 1942 it allowed women to join for the first time.

By 1945, with the war all but over and a majority Labour government in power, the position of trade unions in society had been utterly transformed. The century had begun with a relatively small minority of working people in membership, hostility from employers and constant legal threats. Less than a working lifetime later, the trade union movement was at the centre of public life – a 'fifth estate' deeply tied up in the newly emerging tripartite bodies representing employer, worker and government interests in the corridors of power and numbering among its leaders cabinet ministers and peers of the realm. Could trade unionists ask for anything more?

Union Papers from the Period 1900–1945

The general strike

The TUC Library Collection at **London Metropolitan University** holds an extensive collection of records from the general strike. The collection comprises material collected by library staff in 1926 and includes TUC documents and bulletins, printed publications, and newspapers from Britain and overseas. Other records, such as bulletins produced by local trades councils and strike committees, dispatch riders' reports and photographs, were passed to the Library from other TUC Departments. Further information is available at http://www.london met.ac.uk/services/sas/library-services/tuc.

A selection of material from this collection has been used as the basis for a section of the Union Makes Us Strong website. This includes around 2,000 images including photographs, reports and correspondence and can be found at http://www.unionhistory.info/ generalstrike/index.php.

A further set of records from the strike is held at the **Modern Records**

Centre at **Warwick University**. An index is available here: http://www.warwick.ac.uk/services/library/mrc/ead/292a0200.htm.

The National Archives hold extensive official records, including police reports in series HO 144 with some police records also in MEPO 2. Railway company records can be found in the RAIL series, while Treasury records in T 161 include details of Board of Works employees singled out for advancement or disciplinary action resulting from their involvement in the general strike. Ministry of Labour records are held in LAB 2, Royal Mail records in POST 33 and Ministry of Transport records mostly in MT 45.

An enormous amount of material can be found in local records offices. This is best tracked down through the Access to Archives search engine at http://www.nationalarchives.gov.uk/a2a.

Transport and General Workers' Union

The records of the Transport and General Workers' Union along with those of many of the unions that formed it and have merged into it since its formation in 1922 are held at the **Modern Records Centre** at **Warwick University**. The TGWU is now part of Unite, having merged with the former Amicus trade union in 2007. Published material is fully open, but access to the union's records requires prior written permission. Details for obtaining this are available on the centre's website. For further information see http://www2.warwick.ac.uk/services/library/mrc/archivecatalogues.

National Union of General and Municipal Workers

Following further amalgamations in the 1980s, the National Union of General and Municipal Workers is now known as the GMB. Its archives are held at the **Working Class Movement Library** in Salford and include many important records from the unions that have merged into the GMB over the years. Details of the records found in the GMB Collection can be found at http://www.wcml.org.uk/contents/trade-unions.

Chapter 5

FROM FIFTH ESTATE TO ENEMY WITHIN (1945–1997)

The election of a majority Labour government in 1945 appeared to herald what a later historian of the Labour Party would call a New Jerusalem. The incoming government had 393 MPs and enjoyed a majority of 146 over all other parties combined. In a few short years it was able to take into public ownership the Bank of England (1946), the coal mines (1947), the electricity and gas industries (1948 and 1949), the railways (1948) and the steel industry (1950), while also setting up a National Health Service (1948). By the time it next faced the electorate, the government had nationalized some 20 per cent of the economy and made a further two million people public employees.

Since the British economy had been all but bankrupted by six years of war, all this was no mean achievement, and it largely fulfilled the trade unions' long-standing demands on economic matters. On trade union issues, however, Labour's record in office was less radical. In 1946, the government repealed the Trade Disputes and Trade Unions Act of 1927, allowing civil service trade unions to rejoin the TUC and reintroducing an 'opt out' in place of an 'opt in' arrangement for union political funds. But faced with an economic crisis in 1947 as the impact of Britain's indebtedness to the United States became clear and a harsh winter led to fuel shortages across the country, the government turned towards austerity measures, and in 1948 introduced a wage freeze. The TUC accepted the freeze without enthusiasm, understanding its necessity, but aware of the hostility this would provoke from many rank-and-file members.

Full Employment: The Peaceful Years

The Second World War had transformed the standing of trade unions in British society. The political consensus that emerged included a corporatist approach which favoured involving workers' representatives in decision making, and a commitment to full employment. This was not simply an approach favoured by the 1945 Labour government. It was also endorsed in the then Conservative opposition's *Industrial Charter*, published in 1947, which with its talk of industrial co-partnership and joint production councils set the tone of the party's approach to trade unions for thirty years. The document even proposed a Workers' Charter setting out good practice for employers to follow, with more than a hint that those who failed to do so should not expect to win public sector contracts.

As the austerity of the 1940s gave way to greater prosperity and full employment, the number of trade union members also rose, from just under 8 million in 1945 to pass the 10 million mark in 1962 and on again to 11 million by the end of the decade. Trade union influence in the workplace even began to find a reflection in popular culture – from

Transport and General Workers' Union membership cards from the 1940s to the 1960s. Source: author's collection.

the 1951 Ealing comedy *The Man in the White Suit*, in which managers and unions join forces to prevent the inventor of a new miracle fabric from ruining their industry, to the Boulting brothers' *I'm All Right Jack* of 1959 featuring the actor Peter Sellers' portrayal of change-resistant shop steward Fred Kite.

The 1950s and early 1960s were not entirely without disputes. In 1955 a strike by maintenance engineers and electricians halted national newspaper production for four weeks; the train drivers' union ASLEF brought its members out for a fortnight the same year; and in 1958 bus workers brought London Transport to a halt for seven weeks in a dispute over pay. In all these disputes, however, the TUC attempted to play the role of 'honest broker', seeking a negotiated settlement rather than whipping up support in the wider trade union movement for sympathy strikes. Perhaps the most visible sign of the unions' incorporation into national life, however, came in 1962 when the Conservative government established the National Economic Development Council (swiftly nicknamed Neddie) as a tripartite body of union, employer and government representatives. Neddie would be at the eye of all future economic storms until the Thatcher government sidelined it in the 1980s and it was finally abolished in 1992.

By the end of the 1960s, however, the world of work was changing rapidly – not least because of the rising number of women in employment. In 1968, 850 women machinists at the Ford car factory in Dagenham struck successfully for equal pay. Their campaign inspired the Equal Pay Act of 1970, and opened up a whole new area of industrial relations.

Reorganizing the Unions

While trade union membership cycled through periods of growth and decline throughout the twentieth century, the number of trade unions headed inexorably downwards as mergers and amalgamations led to the creation of fewer, larger organizations (see Appendix 1). Trade union numbers had halved in the first half of the twentieth century, from more than 1,300 at its beginning to fewer than 800 by 1945. The vast number of unions in existence in the early years of the century had proved to be a weakness for trade unionism as a whole. Many small organizations lacked the resources to sustain even a small, localized dispute, were often in dispute with each other over which union had the rights to organize and represent certain groups of workers, and lacked a professional infrastructure. In the wake of the 1926 general strike, the TUC had agreed to encourage union amalgamations, and in 1939 it adopted the Bridlington Principles, which were aimed at preventing unions competing for members or straying into other industries.

Despite a continued programme of amalgamations (in which two unions come together to create a new, third union) and mergers (in which one union is wound up and transfers its engagements to a second, usually larger union), in 1962 the TUC adopted a more aggressive policy of rationalization, sponsoring a series of conferences which set in progress amalgamation or closer working among fourteen groups of unions. As a result, many older unions were to disappear forever, the boilermakers, who could trace their history back to 1834, joining forces with the shipwrights' and blacksmiths' unions in 1963, while the pivotal Amalgamated Engineering Union amalgamated with the foundry workers and draughtsmen in 1971 after many years of negotiations. This process of merger and amalgamation has continued on, through periods of membership rise and fall, through full employment and high unemployment. By 2008, there were just 167 trade unions.

Coupled with this, the decline of old industries and the rise of new, mostly white collar jobs brought about a fundamental shift in trade unionism. The long decline of the Lancashire cotton industry saw the Amalgamated Weavers' Association reduced from some 219,000 members at its peak in the 1920s to just 33,000 by 1968. The miners and railwaymen, also both long-standing stalwarts of the trade union movement, also saw their numbers much reduced. At first the trade union movement was slow to make up these numbers by recruiting elsewhere. During the 1950s and early 1960s, white collar jobs grew at a much faster rate than white collar union membership. However, between 1964 and 1970, white collar union membership grew by more than a third, while the number of white collar jobs increased by less than 5 per cent. By 1979, about 44 per cent of all white collar workers were union members, and 40 per cent of all trade union members were in white collar jobs.

A further shift in trade union organization came about as a result of the Labour government's Royal Commission on Trade Unions. Set up in 1965, the Donovan Commission was intended to address concern about the growing number of unofficial strikes, organized at local level but without the official sanction of union governing bodies. Its report, in 1968, said there were two systems of industrial relations: an official one, in which national union leaders sat down with industry and government but had little real control over what happened on the shop floor, and an unofficial one in which shop stewards wielded real power in the workplace and in negotiations with managers. Its solution, largely adopted over the next few years, was for unions to bring the unofficial shop steward networks within their official structures by providing training and support to local officials, and for a more formal recognition of plant and company level industrial relations.

However, a further government white paper put forward by the Employment Secretary, Barbara Castle, and titled *In Place of Strife*, proved to be too much. Its call for compulsory pre-strike ballots and a central board able to force settlements in industrial disputes provoked in-fighting within the Labour government and the unions and may well have been a factor in the Conservative election victory of 1970.

UNION LIVES: FRANK CHAPPLE (1921–2004)

When Frank Chapple published his autobiography, *Sparks Fly*, his choice of title was particularly apt. Throughout his career, the electricians' union leader had been at the centre of political controversy, and even by his own admission he was 'an awkward bugger'.

Francis Joseph Chapple was born in Hoxton in east London, in a flat above his father's shoe-repair shop. Leaving school at 14, he found work running errands, but soon managed to get himself taken on as an apprentice with an electrical firm. He joined the Electrical Trade Union and became involved in its Islington branch. Although Chapple had already joined the Labour League of Youth, in 1939 he was among a group which defected to the Young Communist League.

Working in the ordnance factories, Chapple could have sat out the Second World War in his reserved occupation, but instead joined the Royal Electrical and Mechanical Engineers. While in the army, he made contact with the German Communist Party, and in 1947 he was sent as an ETU delegate to the World Federation of Democratic Youth – a Communist front organization – in Prague. But both he and his fellow delegate, Les Cannon, became increasingly critical of the Communist Party and the Communist leadership of their own union over the next few years.

Elected to the union's executive in 1957, Chapple soon left the Communist Party and returned to the Labour Party. In 1959 he and Cannon backed Jock Byrne, the right's candidate for general secretary of the ETU. After a bitter fight which the union declared Byrne had lost, the battle went to the High Court, which reversed the decision and uncovered ballot-rigging on a grand scale.

The election and the ruling effectively ended Communist dominance of the ETU, and when Chapple succeeded Byrne as general secretary in 1966, he and Cannon, by now president, changed the union's rules to bar Communists from office and used their considerable organizational skills to embed a right-wing dominance of the union. In 1968, the ETU merged with the Plumbing Trades Union to form the Electrical, Electronic, Telecommunications and Plumbing Union, and two years later, following Cannon's death, Chapple was named both general secretary and president.

As the union's TUC representative after 1970, Chapple strongly criticized union opposition to the Heath Government's industrial relations policies. In 1981 his growing disillusionment with the Labour Party led him to support the breakaway Social Democratic Party. Despite this, he was elected TUC president in 1982. Fiercely critical of the National Union of Mineworkers during their 1984–85 strike, and particularly of its general secretary, Arthur Scargill, Chapple was controversial to the end. He retired in 1984 and was made a life peer by the then Conservative government.

The 1970s: 'Out Brothers, Out ...'

By 1970, the Conservative Party's attitude towards trade unions had undergone a complete reversal. That year's general election brought to power a government committed to cutting trade unions down to size. By the end of the decade, the unions themselves had brought down two governments and their membership numbers were at an all-time high.

In 1971, the Conservative government introduced an Industrial Relations Act which required trade unions to register with a government-appointed body and established a National Industrial Relations Court able to ban strikes and force the settlement of disputes. Led by the TUC, the unions launched a massive campaign to 'Kill the Bill', resulting in a one-day strike by 1.5 million engineering workers and an instruction to member unions to refuse to comply with the law. The Transport and General Workers' Union was fined twice for contempt of court over its refusal to register under the Act, and the conflict came to a head when five dockers' shop stewards were imprisoned for failing to appear before the National Industrial Relations Court. Amid a massive campaign of strikes and protests, the official solicitor eventually went to the prison in person and exercised almost forgotten powers to have the 'Pentonville Five' released.

Forced into retreat on the legal front, the government also suffered defeat at the hands of the National Union of Mineworkers when, in January 1972, 280,000 miners walked out after rejecting a pay offer. Amid power cuts and following the declaration of a state of emergency by the government, they returned to work having wrung an additional 15 per cent out of the National Coal Board at the end of February 1972. Two years later, yet another pay dispute saw the miners out on strike once again. This time, Prime Minister Edward Heath called the unions' bluff and called a general election, asking voters to decide 'Who governs?' The electorate's response was to return Labour's Harold Wilson to power in Heath's place, and after sixteen weeks the miners ended their strike with a 35 per cent pay rise. The Industrial Relations Act was repealed before the end of the year.

The 1970s have a reputation as a period of industrial militancy. By comparison with the previous four decades it is a well-deserved reputation. But in fact the number of days lost to strikes during the decade was never as bad as it had been in the first quarter of the twentieth century. Even so, the success of the unions in winning concessions and pay rises for their members did wonders for recruitment. Between 1970 and the end of the decade, trade union membership rose by nearly 3 million, peaking at 12,947,000 in 1980.

Wilson's government took a more conciliatory approach to trade unions, introducing a right for local union representatives to paid time off work for training in industrial relations and health and safety. But it also had to confront the continuing problem of Britain's industrial decline. The spiral of rising wages being passed on to customers through rising prices made inflation a significant problem, and worsened the difficulties of exporters as British goods were now comparatively expensive. The government tried to address this first through voluntary wage restraint on the part of the unions, and when this failed through a stronger 'social contract' with the TUC which set limits on pay rises. But in the wake of a series of public sector strikes over the winter of 1978–79, the government fell – and the long rise of trade unionism came to a sudden and abrupt halt.

UNION LIVES: JACK JONES (1913–2009)

In January 1977, at the peak of his time in office as general secretary of the Transport and General Workers' Union, a Gallup opinion poll named Jack Jones as the most powerful man in Britain. Jones himself would hardly have seen the finding as a personal accolade, but it is certainly a testimony to the perceived power of the trade union movement at the time – and a measure of the extent to which it transformed the lives of those who rose to high office within it.

The son of a Liverpool docker, Jack Jones – his full name, James Larkin Jones, hinting at his parents' political and trade union sympathies – left school at the age of 14 for an engineering apprenticeship. Influenced by reading Robert Tressell's story of Edwardian socialism, *The Ragged Trousered Philanthropist*, Jones soon joined both the Amalgamated Society of Engineers and the Labour Party.

With the Wall Street Crash of 1929, however, he lost his job and his hopes of an engineering career, and after a period of unemployment joined his father on the docks. In his new job, Jones joined the Transport and General Workers' Union, serving as a shop steward and as a delegate to the TGWU's national docks committee. In 1931 he also became secretary of the Liverpool Labour College.

Following the outbreak of the Spanish Civil War, Jones became involved in the Aid Spain campaign on behalf of the elected republican government, and after hearing a speech by the singer and anti-fascist activist Paul Robeson, he volunteered as a member of the International Brigade. After fighting for some months, he was badly wounded at the Battle of Ebro in July 1938 and returned home.

During the Second World War, Jones worked as a TGWU official on Merseyside before becoming regional secretary in the West Midlands, where he played an important role organizing car workers. Throughout this time Jones was a strong supporter of the shop stewards' movement. Elected TGWU general secretary in 1968, he and Hugh Scanlon of the engineering union led the left opposition to the Labour government's prices and incomes policy, and campaigned vigorously against the reforms to trade union governance proposed by *In Place of Strife*.

As chief economic spokesman for the TUC and a member of the National Economic Development Council, Jones played an influential role in government, and was instrumental in moves to establish the Advisory, Conciliation and Arbitration Service in 1975. Jones retired in 1977, but continued his political activities – as president of both the National Pensioners Convention and, separately, the International Brigade Memorial Trust. His autobiography, *Union Man*, was published in 1986.

Public Service Unions

Public service trade unions were the great success story of the post-war years. The Confederation of Health Service Employees, created through a 1946 amalgamation, increased its membership from fewer than 30,000 at the outset to some 230,000 by the early 1980s. Similarly, the National Union of Public Employees entered the post-war era with 130,000 members and forty years later could claim 690,000, while the National Association of Local Government Officers had 140,000 members in 1946 and 850,000 at its peak in the 1980s. NALGO's expansion had been helped by its decision to join the TUC in 1964, but even unions which remained on the outside benefited. The Royal College of Nursing, which remains outside the TUC today, had 45,355 members in 1948 and had reached 250,000 by the mid-1980s, continuing to grow thereafter. Elsewhere in the public sector, trade unions representing teachers, civil servants and other groups all saw their membership figures take off in the three and a half decades after 1945.

In part the growth in public service trade unionism was a reflection of the fact that there were vastly more jobs in local and national government, education and the public provision of healthcare than there had ever previously been. But public service employers were also more prepared to operate a 'check off' system which allowed union subscriptions to be deducted directly from a member's pay. For the unions this solved the perennial problem that new members would sign up with enthusiasm but eventually cease to pay their subscriptions through apathy. Under check off, apathy worked in favour of continued membership. But the system also meant that most members were increasingly unlikely to take an active part in their union, while the unions were more dependent on employers' assistance. Cut off from the unions' internal decision-taking processes, the views of these largely passive members were often not reflected in the policies put forward by unions' national and local leaderships. Worse, when in 1993 British Rail decided to withdraw check-off facilities, it threatened the National Union of Rail, Maritime and Transport Workers with a potential loss of subscriptions from 85,000 members. It was only saved from financial meltdown by a good computerized membership system and an effective campaign to convince members that they should pay in other ways.

After 1979: Decline and Fall

The Conservative government that came to power in 1979 did not immediately set out on a mission to destroy the unions. Jim Prior, who served as Margaret Thatcher's first Employment Secretary from 1979 to 1981, was often reported to be at odds with his prime minister, who felt he was not sufficiently robust in his approach. But the economic recession that arrived hard on the heels of Mrs Thatcher's entry into 10 Downing Street sent trade union membership into freefall as not just companies but whole industries collapsed. Massive cuts in public

National Union of Mineworkers' banner arrives in Trafalgar Square to support a print workers' march during their 1986 dispute with Rupert Murdoch's News International. Photo: Mark Crail.

spending and the contracting out of many public services to private firms also struck at the heart of the unions in their public sector strongholds. During the course of the 1980s, trade unions lost nearly three million members, and by the early 1990s membership numbers were back to those last seen during the Second World War.

With her own position in power cemented by the removal of cabinet-level opposition within her own party, Mrs Thatcher exploited the unions' weakening position to introduce a raft of new laws. Through a series of Trade Union and Employment Acts, unions now found themselves forced to hold postal ballots before industrial action, to elect their most senior officials at five-yearly intervals, and to hold regular ballots of members over the continued existence of their political funds. All of this made it difficult for unions to act quickly and effectively on behalf of their members. Coupled with their exclusion at national level from any hope of influencing government, they found themselves weaker than at any time since the aftermath of the 1926 general strike. Yet there were a number of unexpectedly beneficial consequences of these reforms – not least in helping to ensure that the leaderships of trade unions became more representative of their members. To give an extreme example, the health union COHSE had previously operated a form of indirect democracy under which members of its national executive were elected by regional delegate conferences of branch activists. As a result, by the mid-1980s, while 80 per cent of the union's members were women, its 26-strong national executive included twenty-three men and there were few female full-time officials. The legal obligation to hold postal ballots of individual members meant that, for the first time, the union had to compile a database of all members and that by the time it amalgamated with NALGO and NUPE in 1993 to create Unison, the majority of its executive and a far higher proportion of its full-time officials were women.

Once again, however, the main point of confrontation between the organized labour movement and a Conservative government was in the coalfields. Early in 1984, the National Coal Board announced that it was planning to close twenty pits with the loss of 20,000 jobs. Strike action began at Manvers in South Yorkshire, with miners at Cortonwood and other collieries in the area soon joining the dispute. Within a week, the National Union of Mineworkers had declared a national strike, and its president, Arthur Scargill, urged members across the country to join it. In the absence of a ballot, many

Twenty-first-century trade unionists march through Tolpuddle to commemorate the trade union martyrs of the early nineteenth century. Photo: Tom Roper.

Nottinghamshire miners refused to halt work, severely weakening the union's position. The government also took a tough line, mobilizing massed ranks of police officers to deny NUM pickets the victories they had been able to achieve in earlier disputes, and declaring the striking miners to be 'the enemy within'. It even used MI5 to tap union leaders' phones. The year-long strike left a bitter legacy within the trade union movement and more generally in the country. But by the time it ended, the NUM was in dire straits, its power broken and its ability to defend its members' jobs destroyed. In due course, pit closures and privatization would reduce NUM membership from more than a quarter of a million in 1979 to just 5,000 thirty years later.

The defeat of the miners was a blow to the morale of the labour movement. This was compounded by the defeat of the print unions in their dispute with News International in 1986, and by the continuing decline in trade union membership. Between 1979 and its eventual merger with Amicus (itself a merger of the engineering unions, print unions and others) in 2007, the Transport and General Workers' Union alone lost more than one million members. And by the time the next Labour government came to power in 1997, overall union membership had declined to just 8 million. Unlike previous Labour governments, this one made few promises to the unions. Although it did deliver some respite from the worst excesses of the union-hostile legislation of the 1980s, its main efforts were focused on improving the lot of working people rather than strengthening their institutions – making it more difficult to dismiss employees, introducing a national minimum wage and improving maternity rights. The effect has been to slow the decline of trade union membership. By 2008, there were a total of 7,628,000 trade union members in 167 trade unions. Whether the future holds a recovery of the sort seen in the mid-1930s or a continued decline into oblivion remains to be seen.

Union Papers from the Period after 1945

Many of the sources mentioned in previous chapters hold trade union papers that extend into the latter half of the twentieth century – most notably the **Modern Records Centre** at **Warwick University**, the **Working Class Movement Library**, the **TUC Library Collections**, and **Bishopsgate Institute**. The following collections are also important.

Royal College of Nursing

RCN Archives, 42 South Oswald Road, Edinburgh EH9 2HH
Tel: 0131 662 6122
Email: archives@rcn.org.uk
The RCN archives are an important source for the study of the history of nursing as well as a rich resource for family historians. The archives are held at the RCN's Edinburgh offices, but researchers should be aware that while the library offers access to RCN council and committee paperwork and to personal papers donated by individuals, membership records are closed. The exception is a published volume covering 1916–23 which gives name, joining date, address and qualification. Further information can be found at http://www.rcn. org.uk/development/library/archives along with a searchable index of the archives at http://rcnarchive.rcn.org.uk and a factsheet on how to trace nurses. **The UK Centre for the History of Nursing and Midwifery** based at the **University of Manchester** is also a good starting point (see http://www.nursing.manchester.ac.uk/ukchnm for further information).

1984–85 miners' strike

A vast wealth of material relating to the 1984–85 miners' strike exists in archives across the country, including papers from some of the many miners' support groups, trade union records and elsewhere. These have been documented in an article on the Archives Hub at http://www.archiveshub.ac.uk/mar04.shtml.

Other archives

Frank Chapple's personal papers are in **Warwick University's Modern Records Centre**. The papers have not yet been catalogued, but a description can be found at http://www.warwick.ac.uk/services/library/mrc/ead/387_6_CHcol.htm.

Archives relating to three former general secretaries of the Transport and General Workers' Union, **Ernest Bevin** (in office 1922–45), **Jack Jones** (1969–78) and the union's first black leader **Bill Morris** (1992–2003) form part of the TGWU archive at the **Modern Records Centre**. Note that researchers must obtain prior permission from Unite, the TGWU's successor union, to examine unpublished material. Personal permission from Lord Morris is required to examine his papers during his lifetime. The papers of Frank Cousins (general secretary 1956–69) can also be found at Warwick – http://www.warwick.ac.uk/services/library/mrc/ead/282.htm.

Further Reading

The *Dictionary of Labour Biography* now runs to twelve volumes. Entries range from lengthy essays on the lives of major political and trade union figures to short entries on local and regional activists. The dictionary includes entries for individuals dating from the 1790s to the modern day. The series is published by Macmillan, while the research papers for it can be found in the Brynmor Jones Library at the University of Hull.

British Trade Unions, 1945–1995 by Chris Wrigley (Manchester University Press, 1997) provides a relatively short but fact-packed account of changes to the trade union movement in the half century after the Second World War, but also includes a selection of extracts from original documents of the period.

The History of the TUC 1869–1968: A Pictorial Survey of a Social Revolution (TUC, 1969) is a celebratory account of the rise of the trade union movement published to mark the TUC's centenary.

Chapter 6

CHARTISM: THE FIRST WORKERS' MOVEMENT

It has been said that, in 1848, when the French overthrew the monarchy and revolutions broke out across Europe, we in Britain organized a petition. Those who lived through the Year of Revolutions saw things rather differently. In Ashton-under-Lyne and other Northern towns, the Chartist National Guard patrolled the streets; there were riots in Trafalgar Square; conspirators armed with pikes and guns were arrested in two London pubs on the very night they planned to seize the city; and 85,000 special constables were sworn in and the army mobilized as defence against the Chartists who gathered on Kennington Common on 10 April before taking their petition to Parliament.

For a decade, from the publication of the People's Charter in 1838 until the late summer of 1848, three great waves of Chartist activity threatened to overthrow the political settlement enshrined in the 1832 Reform Act between the aristocracy and factory-owning classes and to hasten Britain on its way to democracy. The monster petitions organized by the Chartist movement in support of the Six Points of the Charter were supported by a greater number of people than were then entitled to vote in parliamentary elections; in the National Charter Association, supporters of the Charter created the first independent working-class political party anywhere in the world; and through the *Northern Star* and other newspapers, they helped to create a print culture which would leave an unparalleled record of ordinary people's involvement in the struggle for democracy.

This chapter looks at the many and diverse records of Chartism which can enable family historians today to discover their Chartist ancestors and to understand what led them to rally behind the famous Six Points of the Charter:

• A vote for every man over 21
• Secret ballots

- No property qualification
- Payment of MPs
- Constituencies of equal size
- Annual parliaments.

The Missing Records

The most widely known fact about the Chartists is, of course, that they organized a series of massive petitions to Parliament in support of the Charter. There were, in fact, not three petitions, but six. In addition to the best-known petitions of 1839, 1842 and 1848, there was a further petition carrying more than 1.3 million names in 1841 which sought a pardon for those arrested and imprisoned for their Chartist activities, and two much smaller petitions in 1849 and 1851 which carried a few tens of thousands of names and show how quickly Chartism ceased to be a mass movement after 1848.

Sadly for family and indeed all historians, not one of these petitions has survived. After being handed in to hostile parliaments, whose members rejected the demands out of hand, they were consigned to the cellars, and probably destroyed in the fires of the parliamentary boiler rooms, fuelling the central heating systems that warmed Victorian MPs' seats.

Neither is there any membership list for those who joined the National Charter Association. Formed in 1840 and lasting until 1858, the NCA was the largest and most significant Chartist organization, but by no means the only one. Unfortunately, in the political climate of the time, Chartists feared that creating a membership list would in effect provide the authorities with the names of those to be targeted and arrested. In addition, despite the adoption of grandiose organizational schemes and rule books setting out members' rights and obligations, membership was in reality a rather more fluid concept. Some dedicated Chartists might well pay regular subscriptions and hold current membership cards; others would affiliate themselves to a branch of the NCA or a local working men's association, contributing financially as and when they could. Still others, swept up in the excitement of a speech by one of the Chartist movement's great orators, might well take one of the many cards handed out by activists, only to think better of it in the morning.

Finally, a family historian might hope to read the minutes of the NCA's weekly executive committee meetings or those of its hundreds of local branches in the hope of finding their ancestor. For much the same reason that there is no membership list, and because few working-class people had either the space or the opportunity to leave personal archives, these too are lost. Being a Chartist activist risked constant trouble with the law, and few wanted to provide the authorities with documents that could be used to convict them and see them sentenced to long prison terms or transportation. In its issue of 26 November 1842, the *Northern Star* notes that the Hull branch of the NCA was unable to produce documentation sent to its secretary James Grassby because it 'was destroyed along with Mr Grassby's other papers by his wife after he left the district, on her learning that he was included in the "Conspiracy" indictment'.

What Information does Survive?

Although an enormous amount of material has not survived the century and a half since the end of Chartism, it is one of the best researched political movements in history and it is quite possible to locate many thousands of individual supporters and, in a surprisingly large number of cases, to get a very good idea of their political views and activities within the Chartist movement.

Since the Chartist era spanned the best part of two decades, however, it is important to understand the broad phases of its development in order to get a good idea of the sorts of records which might exist and what they are likely to reveal.

The first petition and the Newport rebellion, 1837–40

There are numerous introductory texts which look at the political and economic causes of Chartism. In understanding the roots of the Chartist movement, however, it is important to understand the very different strands that came together in the late 1830s to present such a significant challenge to a parliamentary system which relied for its legitimacy on the votes of a tiny minority of the people.

The Charter and its Six Points were the work of the London Working Men's Association. Formed in 1836, it was one of many overlapping and often short-lived radical organizations in the capital. The LWMA, under the guidance of its secretary William Lovett, had no aspirations to create a mass movement, but hoped to work with the small number of sympathetic MPs to promote its demands – all of which had been a part of the radical programme for the best part of half a century. The use of a petition to promote the cause, meanwhile, emerged from the wealthy middle-class radicals of the Birmingham Political Union, which had been wound up after playing a leading part in the agitation for the 1832 Reform Act but was revived in 1837 primarily to lobby on behalf of workers affected by terrible economic conditions. The vast numbers of primarily Northern working-class supporters who flooded into Chartism fresh from campaigns against the workhouses of the New Poor Law and disillusioned by what they saw as the middle-class betrayal of 1832 which had shut them out of political power were mobilized mainly through the Great Northern Union founded in 1838 by the *Northern Star*. This was published by the former Irish radical MP Feargus O'Connor, who would be the central figure in Chartism until the late 1840s.

Together, these disparate groups, along with the better organized but more cautious Chartists of Scotland, who drew their strength from the Glasgow trade union movement and a tradition of religious dissent, succeeded in 1838 and 1839 in collecting 1,280,958 names on a petition which, according to the *Northern Star*, was three miles (minus 250 yards) in length and weighed six hundredweight or 305kg. Presented to Parliament by the Birmingham MP Thomas Attwood, the petition was duly rejected by a majority of 235 votes to 46, throwing the Chartist movement into confusion. Although not unexpected, MPs' rejection of the petition exposed deep divisions within the ranks of the General Convention of the Industrious Classes, which had been called to finalize its presentation. Some saw it as an alternative Parliament in waiting, and there was much talk of the 'ulterior measures' which would follow the MPs' vote, including a 'sacred month' or general strike, an organized run on the banks, and a policy of 'exclusive dealing' which would see Chartists and their families refuse to use shops and businesses run by their opponents.

As feelings ran high, rioting broke out on the streets of Birmingham, where the Convention had been sitting, and its secretary, William Lovett, was arrested and imprisoned on charges of publishing a seditious libel. But when the Convention dispersed, unable to agree on a strategy and unsure it could command public support for ulterior measures, there was worse to come. In South Wales, an armed mob numbering in the thousands marched on Newport under the command of John Frost, a former mayor of the town and its delegate to the Convention. Soldiers fired on the crowd from the Westgate Hotel and at least twenty were killed in the fighting. Further risings planned

Delegates to the General Convention of the Industrious Classes, 1839, as pictured in
The Charter *newspaper. Source: author's collection.*

for towns and cities across the North of England failed to materialize.
Frost and other leaders were put on trial and initially sentenced to
death. After much lobbying the sentence was commuted to
transportation for life to Australia. Shocked by events, Chartists were
forced to turn their attentions to raising funds for the families of those
imprisoned and transported, and to petitioning for clemency. By
August 1840, official records showed there to be 665 political prisoners
in British jails, almost invariably Chartists. However, out of the ruins of
this first wave of Chartism also emerged the idea for the National
Charter Association as a central co-ordinating body for the cause.

The 1842 petition and general strike

By the time Chartism recovered sufficient of its former confidence to
consider a second petition to Parliament in support of the Six Points,
late in 1841, it had evolved a long way from its roots. The NCA, itself

A medallion issued to mark the release of the Chartist leader Feargus O'Connor from York Castle jail in 1841. Source: author's collection.

dominated by Feargus O'Connor, was now the driving force of a movement which had lost much of its middle-class support and was also beginning to move away from its roots in the radical artisan culture to base itself firmly among factory and mill workers. William Lovett, who while in prison had written a tract calling for education to be placed at the heart of the cause, found himself and his supporters sidelined and attacked for appearing to suggest that the vote was not a right but a privilege for which working men should prove themselves worthy. Nevertheless, with the *Northern Star* putting its weight firmly behind the second petition, it achieved a remarkable 3,315,752 names – an outstanding achievement considering that the adult population of England, Scotland and Wales was under 10 million. This time the petition ran to six miles of paper – twice the length of the first petition. Seven bands accompanied it through London, and the door to the House of Commons had to be dismantled to allow it into the Chamber. Despite this, the petition was again rejected, by 287 votes to forty-nine.

Violence once again followed. Through the summer of 1842, a wave of strikes swept across the Potteries, the North West of England and up to Scotland in protest at employers' attempts to cut wages following a slump in trade. As strikers moved from town to town, removing the plugs from factory boilers to prevent them operating, their demands took on a political edge, with mass meetings adopting declarations that there would be no return to work until the Charter was achieved. An NCA conference, meeting in Manchester, reluctantly put itself at the head of the movement, fearing all the time that it was being set up by the factory owners. Eventually, with troops called in to restore order, the factory workers were forced back to work. Meanwhile, there were hundreds of arrests. In Staffordshire alone, 274 men and women were brought to trial, of whom 146 were imprisoned and fifty-four transported to Australia, mostly as a result of their involvement in riots and the destruction of property. But the authorities also arrested Feargus O'Connor and fifty-eight other Chartists who had either led the strikes or were delegates to the Manchester conference and put them on trial on nine counts of inciting riots, risings, strikes and other forms of disorder. Despite fears that O'Connor and others might face the death sentence, political considerations meant that in the end none of the thirty-nine men found guilty at the trial was ever sentenced.

The land plan

With Chartism once again in the doldrums and many local leaders behind bars, O'Connor and the *Northern Star* turned their attention away from Chartism's traditional political concerns and towards a grandiose scheme for resettling factory workers on smallholdings, which would both give them economic independence and qualify them for the vote. The idea was that thousands of Chartists would contribute small sums to take out a shareholding in a National Land Company. The money would be used to buy estates, which could be divided up into smallholdings, each with its own small cottage. Names would then be drawn from a hat and the successful men and women would become tenants of the company, paying rent and helping to fund further acquisitions of land.

In four years, the National Land Company attracted 70,000 shareholders, raised more than £100,000, and acquired a total of 1,118 acres. The first colony, at Heronsgate, near Watford, was renamed O'Connorville, and others were later established at Lowbands, Snigs End, Minster Lovell and Great Dodford in Worcestershire. However, the whole initiative ended in disaster when company law proved incapable of accommodating such an unusual scheme and doubts were raised about the financial probity of those running it. The result was a lengthy parliamentary inquiry (which ultimately cleared O'Connor of impropriety), the winding up of the company, and much ill-feeling within the Chartist movement. Many of those 'lucky' enough to be allocated land also proved entirely incapable of turning their hand to farming, while the tiny size of the smallholdings was often insufficient to maintain a family.

The 1848 petition

But for the land plan, which enthused thousands of Chartists at a time when direct political action was simply not a viable option, Chartism might have faded away after 1842. Instead, it survived and in 1848 presented what may have been its gravest threat to the established political order. The decision to start a third petition coincided with an outbreak of revolutionary activity across Europe which would see the publication of *The Communist Manifesto* by Karl Marx and Frederick Engels, the overthrow of King Louis Philippe in France and the establishment of the Second Republic, and less successful risings throughout the German states and the Hapsburg Empire.

By 10 April 1848, the day set for a great Chartist March on Parliament to present the petition, both the Chartists and the authorities had convinced themselves that momentous events were about to unfold. That morning, a huge crowd began to gather on Kennington Common in South London, often marching there in huge

National Charter Association membership card.
Source: author's collection.

columns from gathering points throughout the capital, with banners and bands at their head. Though estimates of the size of the crowd have varied widely, a figure of 150,000 is now generally accepted. The authorities, however, were prepared. The aged Duke of Wellington was recalled from retirement to mastermind the defence of the capital. On 8 April the royal family was dispatched to the Isle of Wight for their safety. London's military establishment of 3,300 troops was doubled and emergency rations for ten days were issued. Some 500 troops were moved on the morning of 10 April to protect the South Western Railway Company's goods yard at Nine Elms. More than 1,100 army pensioners were mobilized. Some 85,000 special constables were sworn in, including university students, civil servants, shopkeepers, bankers, William Gladstone and the future Emperor Napoleon III of France, then in exile in England. On the roof of the British Museum, curators and building workers gathered an arsenal of stones to rain down on anyone attacking the building, and sawed through staircase joists to create boobytraps. More importantly, as it turned out, all bridges across the Thames were secured, and processions to Parliament banned.

In future years, it became common to look back on 10 April 1848 as the day Chartism was defeated. Fearing bloody suppression, Feargus O'Connor and the executive of the NCA ended the meeting at Kennington Common with a series of speeches and sent their supporters home. And when O'Connor presented the petition to Parliament, claiming it contained 5,700,000 signatures, he was ridiculed and a counter-claim was made by a parliamentary committee that it did not exceed 1,975,496 names. But at the time, there was little perception that Chartism had been defeated. Throughout the summer, there were reports of men drilling under arms in the streets of northern towns. On 14 August, a confrontation between the Chartist National Guard and police in Ashton-under-Lyne ended in the shooting dead of a police officer. London saw repeated demonstrations. And behind the scenes worse trouble was brewing. That summer a number of leading Chartists met in secret to plan a violent rising which would seize control of a stretch of London running from the Strand to St Paul's, throwing up barriers and seeking to disarm any military force sent against it. Unfortunately for those involved, the plot had been thoroughly infiltrated, and at 6 pm on the night of 16 August, eleven men were arrested at the Orange Tree public house. Later, at 9 pm, thirteen more were held at the Angel in Southwark, and within twenty minutes more a large mob had been dispersed at Seven Dials. For four more days arrests continued and quantities of weapons were discovered and seized. Joseph Ritchie, William Lacey, Thomas Fay, William Cuffay, William Dowling, and later George Bridge Mullins were transported to Australia for life. Fifteen others were imprisoned for up to two years.

After 1848

Chartism never again threatened the authorities. But 1848 was by no means the end of the Chartist movement. Over the next few years, a much diminished National Charter Association adopted a political programme which could only be described as socialist – not in the utopian form advocated in earlier years by the likes of Robert Owen, but of the type advocated by Marx and Engels, both of whom, then living in England, were well known to the Chartist leaders of the time. The move was not entirely popular, with supporters of 'the Charter pure and simple' now ranged against advocates of 'the Charter and something more'. Further defections and divisions in the movement followed.

The NCA struggled on for a further ten years, its influence much reduced. An attempt in 1849 to organize a series of local petitions rather than one big petition succeeded in collecting just 53,816 signatures. Two years later, in 1851, a final attempt to petition Parliament resulted in just 11,834 names. During the 1850s, various efforts were made to revive Chartism. But in 1858, Ernest Jones, who in effect succeeded O'Connor as the movement's leader, eventually declared an end to the campaign for the Six Points, urging supporters to work with middle-class reformers and to take what little they could achieve rather than hoping to win all their demands.

Chartists after Chartism

For a generation of radicals, Chartism had been a life-defining experience. William Henry Chadwick was just 19 years old when he was imprisoned in 1848 for his role in the Ashton-under-Lyne rising. He would go on to raise a family, become an actor, phrenologist and mesmerist, help to found the farm labourers' union of the 1870s, return to politics as an itinerant lecturer for William Gladstone's Liberal Party and campaign for the Labour candidate Will Thorne in the general election of 1906. Yet at his death in 1908, he still styled himself 'the last of the Manchester Chartists' and it was as 'the old Chartist' that he was memorialized on his tombstone.

William Henry Chadwick in later life. Source: *Pages from a Life of Strife* by T P Newbould (1911).

Once the heady days of Chartism were over, many thousands who once saw themselves as Chartists would have settled back into everyday life, content to leave politics to other people. But many of those who cut their political teeth on the Six Points of the Charter would go on to other causes. Some ended up in the new Liberal Party that emerged at the end of the 1850s, and for decades the Liberal Party itself sought to lay claim to a sanitized version of Chartism in its own family tree. A photograph taken in 1913 of two aged Chartist veterans holding vicious-looking Chartist pikes from half a century earlier, then in the possession of Failsworth Liberal Club, is a sharp reminder of the change in the political climate since the days of 1848. Even Ernest Jones, the principled leader of Chartism's socialist wing and close associate of Karl Marx and Frederick Engels, would eventually throw in his lot with the Liberals, dying just as he seemed likely to win election to Parliament as a Liberal candidate.

Others moved on into single-issue campaigns – most notably in campaigns for state-funded schools, for the repeal of newspaper taxes, and in later efforts to broaden the franchise. There would be no extension of the vote until 1867, by which time many of the older and more experienced Chartists were old men. The journalist and former Chartist W E Adams would later recall seeing John Arnott, once general secretary of the National Charter Association, in the Strand some time around 1865, by which time he was 'a poor half-starved old man' seeking to beg or borrow a few coppers from a bookseller. Yet two years later Arnott could still manage to pen lyrics to a song to mark a mass meeting of the Reform League. Despite the League's success in 1867, Arnott himself would not benefit. Impoverished and unable to make a living even from begging, he died the following year in St Pancras Workhouse at the age of 68.

Some former Chartists fared rather better. Thomas Martin Wheeler, another former general secretary of the NCA, founded and proved to be a highly capable manager of the Friend-in-Need insurance company until his death in 1862. Abel Heywood, a veteran of the unstamped press whose Manchester print firm had published numerous Chartist pamphlets, would go on to serve twice as mayor of Manchester while his business continued to produce tourist guides for decades to come. On a slightly smaller scale, a business set up with the support of Ashton-under-Lyne Chartists by John Williamson in the 1830s cannily switched from printing tracts on guerrilla warfare to train and bus tickets. It continued as a family business until finally taken over some time in the 1970s.

Among those who quit the UK for good after their involvement in Chartism, Alan Pinkerton, who left Glasgow 'in a hurry' in 1842, went on to found the most famous detective agency in the United States. William Carnegie left Scotland for Pittsburgh with his family in 1848 'on the proceeds from the sale of his four hand-looms'. His son Andrew would go on to become one of the richest men in the world. The former Chartist Henry Parkes would rise to become premier of New South Wales five times between 1872 and 1891 and to be knighted. And finally, Henry Clubb, who had been secretary of the Colchester Working Men's Association, would eventually become a Michigan state senator. It was not until his death in 1921 that it could truly be said that we had seen the last of the Chartists.

Chartist Sources and Archives

The *Northern Star* was the principal Chartist newspaper throughout the period, appearing from 1837 to 1852. Its extensive coverage of local and national Chartist activity makes it an essential source for family historians. A complete run of the paper has been digitized and can be freely accessed online at http://www.ncse.ac.uk/index.html.

A digital version of the *Northern Star* is also available as part of the Gale/Cengage Learning collection of Nineteenth Century British Newspapers. Other Chartist newspapers in the collection include *Charter*, *Chartist*, *Chartist Circular*, *Northern Liberator*, *Southern Star* and *Reynolds's Newspaper*. The collection is generally available only through subscribing academic libraries, but can be accessed at the **National Archives** at Kew. A number of Chartist newspapers have been reissued in modern times in bound volumes. These include *The Chartist Circular* (Augustus M Kelley, 1968), *The English Chartist Circular* (Augustus M Kelley, 1968) and, in two volumes, *The Red Republican* and *The Friend of the People* (Merlin Press, 1966).

The names of subscribers to the Chartist Land Company were recorded in a register submitted by the directors as part of its application to be listed as a limited company. The register survives in the National Archives in BT 41/474/2659, with a supplementary list in BT 41/476/2659. The documents, both now very fragile, list name, occupation and address. Names appear alphabetically by the initial letter of the surname but are not in order within each letter. The names of more than 5,000 subscribers from Lancashire can be found on the Chartist Ancestors website at http://www.chartists.net/Chartist-land-company.htm. The names of those allocated land under the scheme can be found at http://www.chartists.net/Chartist-Land-Plan-1845-50.htm.

Chartist Ancestors website, to be found at www.chartists.net.

The Chartist Ancestors website also includes the names of contributors to Chartist causes and newspapers, members of Chartist organizations, delegates to Chartist conventions, and Chartists arrested, tried and imprisoned in the course of their political activities.

Many of those involved in Chartism would later write about their experiences, and a number of these books have been digitized and published online in recent years, including some of the works of Thomas Cooper, George Jacob Holyoake, W E Adams and John James Bezer. Links to these full-text online titles can be found at http://www.chartists.net/Further-research.htm, although most of the books themselves have been transcribed for the Minor Victorian Poets and Authors website (at http://www.gerald-massey.org.uk) or as part of the Google Books project.

The National Archives has a wealth of material on Chartism, particularly relating to police, court and prison records. A list can be found at http://www.chartists.net/Chartist-archives.htm. In addition, an enormous volume of material can be found in local records offices and archives. This material can be located using the Access to Archives search at http://www.nationalarchives.gov.uk/a2a.

The Dorothy Thompson Collection at Staffordshire University includes 300 books and pamphlets plus Dr Thompson's own research notes on the history of Chartism. Further information can be found by visiting http://www.staffs.ac.uk and searching on the term 'Dorothy Thompson'. The university is also home to the Centre for the Study of Chartism.

Further Reading

Chartism: A New History, Malcolm Chase (Manchester University Press, 2007)

Feargus O'Connor: A Political Life, Paul A Pickering (Merlin Press, 2008)

Voices of the People: Democracy and Chartist Political Identity, Robert G Hall (Merlin Press, 2007)

Papers for the People: A Study of the Chartist Press, ed. Joan Allen and Owen R Ashton (Merlin Press, 2005)

Friends of the People: Uneasy Radicals in the Age of the Chartists, Owen R Ashton and Paul A Pickering (Merlin Press, 2002)

London Chartism 1838–1848, David Goodway (Cambridge University Press, 1982)

Chartism and the Chartists in Manchester and Salford, Paul A Pickering (Macmillan, 1995)

Chapter 7

THE LABOUR PARTY AND ITS FOREBEARS

Twenty years passed between the final demise of Chartism and the emergence of the first explicitly socialist political parties capable of national organization. From these early beginnings grew the Labour Party that we know today, and a host of smaller parties – some still with us, the others long since vanished. The next two chapters will look at the history of the political wing of the labour movement and its records.

This chapter deals with the Labour Party itself and with the parties that played a part in its creation at the turn of the twentieth century. Chapter 8 deals with those other left-wing parties generally seen as forming a part of the wider labour movement. The distinction is not a clear one: the Communist Party of Great Britain (dealt with in Chapter 8) has a better claim of parentage on the Social Democratic Federation than the Labour Party. But it makes sense to include the SDF in the present chapter because, without it, the early history of the Labour Party itself makes little sense.

It is also worth keeping in mind that the left has always been prone to political splits and schisms, with the resulting groups often merging or subdividing further. Over the years this has produced a bewildering array of often small and short-lived parties, some of which refused even to admit to their own existence, preferring to describe themselves as supporters of particular left-wing newspapers. These chapters can only hope to nod an acknowledgement that this multitude of parties existed and to focus on those which made a sustained difference to the labour movement over a period of years.

Social Democratic Federation

On 2 March 1881, the journalist Henry Hyndman convened a meeting of London radicals at the Rose Street Club in Soho. Out of this event arose the Democratic Federation – the first socialist party ever established in Britain. The federation succeeded early on in recruiting a number of veteran Chartists to its cause, and would later bring into membership Eleanor Marx, youngest daughter of Karl Marx and the guardian of his work; the designer and artist William Morris; and George Lansbury, later to be leader of the Labour Party.

In 1884, the federation merged with the London-based Labour Emancipation League, which had grown out of the secularist movement, to form the Social Democratic Federation – the name under which the party is best known. It also began publication of *Justice*, a newspaper which continued long after its supporters split from the SDF in 1916. Although it was now an avowedly Marxist organization, both William Morris and Eleanor Marx left the SDF that same year to form the Socialist League, accusing the SDF of reformism and chauvinism. It would not be the last time such charges were levied against Hyndman, or the last time it lost members to the left.

Leading trade unionists, including John Burns and Tom Mann, also believed that the SDF neglected industrial struggle, and left in 1890. To the right, the SDF lost further members to the Independent Labour Party after its success in getting James Keir Hardie elected for West Ham South in the 1892 general election. In 1895, it would contest four parliamentary seats, losing badly in all of them. Subsequently both Ben Tillett and George Lansbury, one of the four defeated SDF candidates, were among those who defected to the ILP.

In February 1900, the SDF was among the organizations which agreed to Keir Hardie's call to establish 'a distinct Labour group in Parliament'. This led to the setting up of the Labour Representation Committee run by a committee appointed by the SDF, ILP, Fabian Society and trade unions, and would eventually act as midwife to the new Labour Party.

The SDF changed its name in 1907 to become the Social Democratic Party. Four years later it became the British Socialist Party, and managed to draw in a number of small socialist groups, including some grouped around *The Clarion* newspaper and branches of the ILP. In 1914, the party voted to affiliate to the Labour Party, but was also split over its attitude to the First World War. Hyndman, a strong nationalist, supported the war, and would eventually leave the party he founded in 1916 to set up a National Socialist Party.

Inspired by the Bolshevik revolution in Russia, the BLP decided to transform itself into a fully fledged Communist Party, which it did in

1920. Its only MP, a former Liberal by the name of Cecil L'Estrange Malone, had joined just a few months before this final change.

Further research

The **International Institute of Social History in Amsterdam** has a microfilm collection of the SDF's publications. It is listed at http://www.iisg.nl/archives/en/files/s/10769567.php. Archives for the Socialist League can be also found at the institute. These include correspondence, minutes, and lists of those present at conferences. See http://www.iisg.nl/archives/en/files/s/10769755.php.

The **Working Class Movement Library** holds pamphlets produced by the SDF. These are listed, along with others published by the Twentieth Century Press at http://www.wcml.org.uk/holdings/sdf_20thc_byauthor.htm.

A limited number of papers relating to the SDF can be found in the library of the **London School of Economics**. They are listed at http://library-2.lse.ac.uk/archives/handlists/SDF/SDF.html.

Very few of the records produced by the SDF's local branches appear to have survived; however, **Bolton Archive and Local Studies Service** has the Bolton SDF and Bolton Socialist Party minute book and other material. See http://www.bolton.gov.uk for details.

The only recent book-length study of the SDF is Martin Crick's *History of the Social-Democratic Federation* (Keele University Press, 1994).

Fabian Society

Founded on 4 January 1884 by members of an apolitical club known as the Fellowship of the New Life, the Fabian Society swiftly established itself as an intellectual powerhouse for the gradualist and reformist wing of the left. Named after the Roman general Quintus Fabius Maximus, whose policy of harassing the enemy rather than attacking head-on earned him the nickname 'the delayer', the Fabian Society has throughout its history provided a focus for the labour movement's moderate middle-class activists – and as a constant source of policy initiatives and ideas.

The Fabian Society soon attracted many well-known figures in the late Victorian and Edwardian reform movements, including H G Wells, George Bernard Shaw, Virginia Woolf, Emmeline Pankhurst – and most of all Sidney and Beatrice Webb, whose lifelong commitment to social change led them to serve on royal commissions, launch the *New*

THE WAGES OF MEN & WOMEN: SHOULD THEY BE EQUAL ? . .
By Mrs. SIDNEY WEBB.

Published by the Fabian Society at the Fabian Bookshop, 25, Tothill Street, Westminster, S.W.1 ; and by George Allen & Unwin, Ltd., 40, Museum Street, London, W.C.1. Price ONE SHILLING net.

The cover of a 1916 Fabian Society pamphlet by Beatrice Webb poses the question: 'The wages of men and women: should they be equal?'
Source: author's collection.

Statesman, set up the London School of Economics, produce the first History of Trade Unionism and, in Sidney's case, serve as a minister in the Labour government of 1929.

In the 1890s the Fabian Society followed a policy of 'permeation' (with members joining any organization which would have them to promote their ideas) and although it refused to become part of the new Independent Labour Party, it was involved in the launch of the Labour Representation Committee in 1900. At its first conference, it claimed a membership of 861 members, entitling it to one delegate. In 1918, Sidney Webb would write a constitution for the Labour Party, whose famous Clause IV committed it to the 'common ownership of the means of production, distribution and exchange' until it was repealed in 1995.

Between the two world wars, the Fabian Society continued to attract left-leaning intellectuals, including the philosopher R H Tawney and the political theorist and economist G D H Cole. Many future leaders of the post-colonial world also came into contact with Fabianism at this time, often while studying in England. Among those influenced by it were India's first prime minister, Jawaharlal Nehru, and the founder of Pakistan, Muhammad Ali Jinnah, who had been an active member of the Fabian Society in the 1930s. The Fabian Society is still active today, and remains affiliated to the Labour Party. It has several thousand members.

Further research

Extensive archives for the Fabian Society are held at the **London School of Economics**. They are also held on microfilm at the **International Institute of Social History in Amsterdam**. These include minute books with related documents, 1884–1918; minutes of the executive committee, 1919–60 and texts of lectures; correspondence; early documents; records of the finance and general purposes committee, 1919–64, the publications committee, 1914–64, Fabian local societies, 1941–64, the women's group, 1919–51, the Society for Socialist Inquiry and Propaganda, 1931–32, the New Fabian Research Bureau, 1931–39, and other related bodies.

Independent Labour Party

From the late 1880s onwards, an increasing number of small local groups sprang up to promote the cause of independent labour movement representation in Parliament. At the general election of 1892, they made their breakthrough, winning three seats independently of the Liberal Party, whose patronage had brought the first Lib-Lab MPs into Parliament. Of the three, however, just one – James Keir Hardie – appeared willing to take an independent socialist line, and meeting at the Trades Union Congress of that year, a group of activists agreed to convene a national conference with the aim of establishing a Labour Party.

The conference met at Bradford on 13 and 14 January 1893. Keir Hardie was in the chair, and there were 124 delegates, most of whom came from the industrial towns of the North of England. Among those present were delegates from branches of both the Fabian Society and the Social Democratic Federation, but many others represented purely local socialist societies. Within months these had been transformed into branches of the ILP, although the new party's centralized structure meant that there was no place for trade unions or other groups, including the Fabians, to sign up as affiliates.

The early history of the ILP is patchy. Delegate numbers at annual conferences fell from 124 at Bradford in 1893 to just ninety-three at Manchester in 1894 and eighty-nine in Newcastle in 1895, but this is not the whole picture as many smaller branches could not afford to send delegates. Similarly, Keir Hardie had originally claimed in 1895 that the ILP had 35,000 members, but this was reduced to 20,000 by the party's council the following year, and even this appears to have been an exaggeration.

The party was active in fighting by-elections, however, and at the 1895 general election, the ILP fielded twenty-eight candidates, including eight in Lancashire and Cheshire, seven in Yorkshire and seven in Scotland. None was successful, with Keir Hardie losing his seat in South West Ham, and his two former Independent Labour colleagues in the Commons joining the ranks of the Lib-Labs. It was clear by the turn of the century that the ILP was not on its way to becoming a mass Labour Party. But despite these setbacks, by 1900 the ILP had sixty-three town councillors, four county councillors, thirty-six urban and four rural district councillors, sixteen parish councillors, eight citizens' auditors, fifty-one members on boards of poor law guardians, and sixty-six on school boards.

The next venture in which the ILP became involved, however, transformed the face of British politics. In February 1900, a conference called by the TUC at which the ILP and other left parties were represented agreed to establish a Labour Representation Committee, to win wider working-class representation in Parliament and to co-ordinate the work of existing trade union MPs. James Ramsay MacDonald, a leading ILP figure, became the LRC's first secretary. The LRC's electoral success led to the creation in 1906 of the Labour Party, to which the ILP was also affiliated. But since it was not possible to become an individual member of the new party until 1918, most activists across the country were in practice ILP members.

The ILP remained affiliated to the Labour Party throughout the 1920s and its early experiences of government. But as the left of the ILP came to be increasingly at odds with the Labour leadership, tensions between the parties grew until, at the 1931 general election, ILP candidates refused to accept the standing orders of the Parliamentary

Labour Party and stood without official Labour endorsement. Just five ILP members were elected, and the party subsequently voted to end its affiliation to the Labour Party – a decision described by the Labour left-winger Aneurin Bevan as a decision to remain 'pure, but impotent'.

In the years that followed, the ILP suffered a massive loss of membership, both to the Labour Party on its right, and to the Communist Party on its left. One group even formed a Revolutionary Policy Committee, advocating a merger with the Communist Party. In 1935 its leading members defected as a group. At the same time, the emerging Trotskyist groups on the British left took an interest in the ILP. Leon Trotsky himself urged supporters in the Marxist Group to join the ILP to work for the 'Bolshevik transformation of the party'.

The ILP had one further claim to historical significance, however. Its members formed the core of an International Brigade who travelled to Spain in 1937 to fight for the Republican cause against General Franco's fascists. The best known of these International Brigaders was the writer George Orwell, but others included the future trade union leader Jack Jones and the Labour MP Bob Edwards. Although not all were ILP members, there were a total of 2,100 British volunteers for the Republican cause, 526 of whom died. A memorial to them now stands on London's South Bank.

At the 1945 general election in the wake of the Second World War, the ILP held on to a handful of seats. But after the death of its leader James Maxton in 1946, its remaining MPs defected to the Labour Party. The ILP never won another parliamentary election, but struggled on through the 1950s and 1960s regardless, with a declining and ageing membership. In 1975, it renamed itself Independent Labour Publications and its members rejoined the Labour Party.

Further research

The **London School of Economic and Political Science** has an extensive collection of archival material from the ILP in its library's archives division. The collection runs to 263 boxes and includes the minutes of the National Administrative Council, head office papers and some branch records. An online catalogue which also describes the structure and organization of the ILP can be found at http://library-2.lse.ac.uk/archives/handlists/ILP/ILP.html.

Records for many ILP branches have survived in **local records offices**. A search in the National Register of Archives reveals the location of eighty-four collections. Go to http://www.national archives.gov.uk/nra/default.asp and search on the term 'Independent Labour Party'.

The **International Brigade Memorial Trust** provides an excellent starting point for discovering more about the volunteers who fought for the Republican cause in the Spanish civil war. Its website at http://www.international-brigades.org.uk also provides links to further sources.

Labour Party

Formed at a conference in 1900 called by the Trades Union Congress, the Labour Representation Committee was, from the start, an attempt to build a broad coalition between the socialist parties, which had provided much of the intellectual vigour on the left, and the trade unions, which had provided the money, organizational ability and sheer weight of membership numbers. The LRC was organized along federal lines. Existing organizations, such as the Fabian Society and Independent Labour Party, were able to affiliate to it, but it was not possible at this stage for individuals to become members. The same structure would be retained after 1906, when the LRC transformed itself into the Labour Party after taking twenty-nine seats at that year's general election.

Postcard of the Labour group in Parliament after the 1906 general election. With twenty-nine MPs and Keir Hardie (seated, centre) as leader, the Labour Representation Committee now reconstituted itself as the Labour Party. Source: author's collection.

Lacking a mass membership of its own, much of the politics of the early Labour Party was played out within the affiliated socialist organizations and trade unions, and between them. Come the outbreak of war in 1914, the party was deeply divided, with many socialists around the ILP and the British Socialist Party, which had now belatedly agreed to affiliate, opposed to war. ILP members including a young Fenner Brockway, later to become a Labour cabinet minister, would also oppose conscription and be imprisoned for their activities. Once the war began, however, the bulk of the party leadership gave their support to the Liberal government and some were invited to join Prime Minister David Lloyd George's wartime coalition government.

Out of the war, and with an electorate greatly enlarged by the extension of the franchise in 1918, emerged a new sense that the Labour Party could make a real political breakthrough. Although this was only partially borne out by the results of the general election that year, significant figures within the party, including Arthur Henderson, a trade unionist who had served in Lloyd George's war cabinet, realized that the party needed a new constitution that would bind the political and trade union wings of the party together more closely and bring into membership middle-class voters who were usually not trade union members. The new constitution, drafted by the Fabian intellectual Sidney Webb, for the first time threw open membership to individuals.

The Labour Party structure put in place in 1918 remained pretty much unchanged for the remainder of the century. At its apex stood the annual party conference, the supreme policy-making body to which local party bodies, trade unions and other affiliated organizations such as the Fabian Society sent delegates. From this body was elected a National Executive Committee, with reserved seats for the local parties, unions and affiliated organizations, plus a number reserved specifically for women to contest. This NEC governed between conferences and shared responsibility with the Parliamentary Labour Party for drawing up the party's programme and the manifesto under which it would contest elections. Since the positions of leader and deputy leader of the Labour Party were elected solely by Labour MPs until the 1980s, no party leader from James Keir Hardie in 1900 through to Michael Foot in 1983 had any official role within the party conference until then. In practice, there was for many years a convention that the party leader addressed the conference each year, but as late as the economic crisis of the Callaghan years the then Chancellor of the Exchequer Denis Healey had to hope that the conference chair would call him to speak from the floor of conference.

Below national level the most significant building block of party organization was the constituency party. Lacking a national membership list, the party required all would-be members to join a constituency Labour Party, which made its own decisions on whom to admit or reject, and reported its decisions to head office. Like the party conference in miniature, constituency parties were governed by committees of delegates from local party branches (the most basic unit of party organization), union branches and any affiliated local socialist societies. These general committees also reserved seats for women members and young members. In some cases, constituency parties grew large and wealthy enough to employ full-time officials to carry out organizational tasks, lead fund-raising and act as the agent for the Labour candidate at election time. Most, however, relied on volunteers. Between these two levels there were (and still are) regional parties, with their own executives and annual conferences but, in most cases, little real power. Scotland, Wales and, to some extent, Greater London were always an exception to this rule, with regional party organization providing a real focus for activity and policy-making.

The Labour Party which put this new constitution into effect had been shaped by two world-shaking events: a world war which gave some at least of its leaders a taste of government office; and a revolution in Russia which forced many on the left to make a choice between their commitment to constitutional politics and solidarity with fellow socialists. So, when the newly formed Communist Party of Great Britain applied to affiliate in 1920, Labour's National Executive Committee turned it away on the grounds that the CPGB's aims were not in accord with the 'constitution, principles and programme' of the Labour Party. Two years later, Henderson's approach to party organization would prove successful when at the 1922 general election Labour succeeded in fielding candidates in 414 constituencies and winning 142. Labour remained essentially an urban political party. As late as 1921 it had organized district parties in only forty-five of the 203 rural constituencies. But for the first time it had won more votes and more seats than a now divided Liberal Party.

As the 1920s went on, the Labour Party leadership found it increasingly necessary to tighten party discipline. The *Labour Herald* newspaper now came under the joint ownership of the Labour Party and TUC, but the real internal battle was with supporters of the new Communist Party. Successive party conferences voted to bar individual

Postcard showing the Labour cabinet of 1929. Although short-lived, it boasted the first woman cabinet minister in Margaret Bondfield. Source: author's collection.

Communist Party members from becoming individual members of the Labour Party, but in 1927 the National Executive Committee had to step in to disband twenty-seven constituency parties that had been infiltrated and taken over by Communist sympathizers.

In the meantime, the hung general election of 1923 saw Labour take 191 seats. The Conservatives, though still the largest party, were unable to continue in government, their policies having been soundly rejected by the electorate, and Labour, though only the second largest party, was given its chance of office. The new administration depended on Liberal support and did not survive long, but it had demonstrated Labour's ability to govern. Six years later, at the 1929 general election, Labour would return to government having become, for the first time, the largest party in the House of Commons. The government was beset by difficulties. Struggling with an economic crisis, it was unable to rely on the support of the Liberals for its legislative programme and faced determined opposition both from the aristocratic Labour MP and later fascist leader Oswald Mosley and his supporters (who would be expelled in 1930 after forming their New Party), and the ILP, which was determined to force its MPs to follow ILP conference policies rather than those of the Labour Party.

In 1931, Labour faced its darkest hour. Struggling with an international financial crisis, Prime Minister James Ramsay MacDonald and his Chancellor Philip Snowden were determined to cut civil service pay and unemployment benefits. Unable to carry his cabinet with him, MacDonald resigned and was immediately asked to form a new coalition government with the support of the Liberals. Once the immediate crisis had passed, it was clear that MacDonald had a mere handful of supporters from the Labour ranks, but his actions sidelined the Labour Party itself and left it out of office for a decade. In the 1930s, effective power within the Labour Party now passed to the unions, and in particular to Ernie Bevin, general secretary of the giant Transport and General Workers' Union, who had the largest vote at the party's annual conference and effectively controlled the line of the million-selling *Daily Herald*. But with the loss of the ILP after its disaffiliation, the Labour left needed a new focus around which it could regroup. It found this focus in the Socialist League, under the leadership of Stafford Cripps, and, from 1937, the closely allied *Tribune* newspaper. The league was affiliated to the Labour Party, but its opposition to the leadership over a range of issues, not least its desire to create a 'united front' against fascism with the ILP and Communist Party, led to a conference vote to eject it.

Having argued since 1937 for rearmament against the growing menace posed by the Nazi regime in Germany, the Labour Party was not as divided at the outbreak of the Second World War as it had been in 1914. It declared an immediate electoral truce, but remained highly critical of the Conservative government's conduct of the war and refused to join a national government under Neville Chamberlain. With Winston Churchill's appointment as prime minister, however, Labour leader Clement Attlee sought the views of both the Labour National Executive Committee and the party conference and accepted the offer of a wartime coalition.

Labour's experience of government in wartime would shape its attitude for the best part of forty years. With Attlee as Deputy Prime Minister, Bevin as Minister of Labour effectively directing the war economy and the allocation of manpower, and Herbert Morrison as Home Secretary, senior Labour figures were now at the centre of a highly centralized government able to command and shape the economy and the country. The 1945 general election that saw Labour sweep to power as a majority government for the first time saw a continuation of this approach, as the new administration established a National Health Service, nationalized the coal and rail industries and vastly extended the scope of the public sector. However, even with a record 14 million votes at the general election of October 1951, Labour lost office and was returned to opposition.

Though the economic crises of the 1930s had passed, the 'thirteen wasted years' that followed Labour's defeat inevitably saw fresh strife between left and right in the party – most notably over rearmament and nuclear weapons. Under the leadership of Aneurin Bevan and *Tribune*, the Labour left fought on throughout the 1950s, with party conferences and internal elections for party office as their battlegrounds. Labour would not return to government until 1964, after the deaths of both Bevan and Hugh Gaitskell, his rival on the Labour right and eventually leader of the party. When it did so, it had at its head Harold Wilson, a former Bevanite who proved adept at positioning himself and his party to catch the electorate's desire for change and political rejuvenation. Wilson would go on to win the general election of 1966, lose office to the Conservatives in 1970 and return triumphant at the elections of February and October 1974. When his successor, James Callaghan, lost to the Conservatives under

The Labour Party's annual conference in Blackpool in 1986. Photo: Mark Crail.

Margaret Thatcher in 1979, Labour once again faced a lengthy period in opposition and a return to internal warfare. The party would not take office again until 1997.

Further research

Minutes and other papers of the Labour Representation Committee are held at the **London School of Economics and Political Science**. These can be located using the library's online catalogue at http://catalogue.lse.ac.uk.

The Labour Party's own archives can be found in the **Labour History Archive and Study Centre** in Manchester (http://www.phm.org.uk). There are also personal archives relating to important Labour Party figures including Arthur Henderson, Eric Heffer, Ian Mikardo, Michael Foot and Jo Richardson. The centre's catalogue can be searched using the **Access to Archives** service at http://www.nationalarchives.gov.uk/a2a. At the time of writing, both the study centre and the People's History Museum, which displays many of the most important items in the collection, are in the process of being rebuilt. They are due to reopen in late 2009.

The records of many local Labour Party organizations can be found in local records offices. Again, the best starting point is the Access to Archives service.

The *Dictionary of Labour Biography* has entries for thousands of significant Labour Party figures, including both MPs and others active in the party. Additionally, former cabinet ministers including Barbara Castle and Tony Benn published extensive though edited versions of their **political diaries** after leaving office. The papers on which Barbara Castle based her published diaries are held by **Bradford University Library** (see http://www.archiveshub.ac.uk/news/0602castle.html). The papers of the socialist theorist Tony Crosland, who held a series of offices in the Labour governments of the 1960s and 1970s are in the **London School of Economics and Politics**. The LSE also holds the papers of Sidney and Beatrice Webb. The **Bodleian Library** (http://www.ouls.ox.ac.uk/bodley) at Oxford has the papers of Clement Attlee, Harold Wilson and James Callaghan.

Numerous Labour MPs have been the subject of biographies. Among the best are:

Harold Wilson, by Ben Pimlott (Harper Collins, 1992)
Callaghan: A Life, by Kenneth O Morgan (Oxford University Press, 1997)

Clem Attlee, by Francis Beckett (Politicos Publishing, 2007)
Keir Hardie: Radical and Socialist, by Kenneth O Morgan (Weidenfeld & Nicolson, 1997)
Red Queen: The Authorised Biography of Barbara Castle, by Anne Perkins (Macmillan, 2003)
Michael Foot: A Life, by Kenneth O Morgan (HarperPress, 2007)
Nye Bevan: A Biography, by John Campbell (Metro Books, 1997).

Labour's rise to power

General election	Votes	MPs	Outcome
1900	62,698	2	Conservative government
1906	321,663	29	Liberal government
Jan. 1910	505,657	40	Minority Liberal government
Dec. 1910	371,802	42	Minority Liberal government
1918	2,245,777	57	Conservative–Liberal government
1922	4,076,665	142	Conservative government
1923	4,267,831	191	First minority Labour government
1924	5,281,626	151	Conservative government
1929	8,048,968	287	Minority Labour government
1931	6,339,306	52	National government
1935	7,984,988	154	National government
1945	11,967,746	393	First majority Labour government

Chapter 8

LEFT MARCH: THE CPGB AND OTHER ORGANIZATIONS

Communist Party of Great Britain

When the Bolsheviks seized power in Russia in October 1917, Britain was still without a communist party of its own. Divided over their attitude towards Labour Party affiliation and to participation in elections, the country's communists were split between numerous small, local groups and rather fewer organizations with some claim to national reach. All this changed in 1919 when the Moscow-based Communist International (also known as the Third International) urged communists around the world to unite and laid down a clear demarcation line between communist and socialist parties.

The Communist Party of Great Britain, founded at a conference in London over the weekend of 31 July to 1 August 1920, had at its core the British Socialist Party (see Chapter 7). However, it also brought into membership a large section of the Socialist Labour Party, which had split from the Social Democratic Federation in 1903 and now claimed to have nearly 1,000 members, and the South Wales Socialist Society, which had a large membership among the miners. In January 1921, following a personal intervention from Moscow by Lenin himself, the party was 'refounded', with the small Scottish-based Communist Labour Party and Sylvia Pankhurst's Communist Party (British Section of the Third International) joining the CPGB.

Following a line set by Lenin, the new party initially tried to affiliate to the Labour Party. When its approaches were rebuffed, the party urged its members to join as individuals and to hold dual membership. As a result, a number of CPGB members became Labour parliamentary candidates, and at the 1922 general election two were elected as MPs.

As a serious revolutionary party and with industrial and political unrest widespread, life was not easy for members of the CPGB, and on the eve of the 1926 general strike many of its leaders were arrested. Although twelve of their number were charged with seditious conspiracy and sentenced to prison terms of between six months and a year, the party played a significant part both in the general strike and supporting the miners who remained out on strike for many months afterwards. As a result, the CPGB was able to grow substantially, particularly in the mining communities but also among other industrial groups. The CPGB had also founded the National Unemployed Workers' Movement, which mobilized thousands and was behind many of the jobless marches of the 1930s.

But with the leadership of world communism having passed to Josef Stalin, the CPGB now adopted an isolationist policy which saw thousands of members desert the party. In the 'third period' of the early 1930s, and under instructions from Moscow, the CPGB's 'class against class' approach led it to declare that workers were as much under threat from other socialist parties as from openly fascist groups. At the same time, it tried – with limited success – to set up 'red unions', under the control of the CPGB and in direct competition with existing trade unions. With the rise of Hitler to power in Germany, and again under orders from Moscow, the party flipped to a diametrically opposed line from 1934, favouring instead a 'popular front' which would unite all anti-fascist opinion, taking the CPGB into alliance not just with willing Labour Party members but also many far to the right of the Labour Party itself.

This new approach proved popular, and at the 1935 general election, Willie Gallacher was elected as MP for West Fife, giving the CPGB its first parliamentary voice in six years. Communist Party members also played a leading role in the Battle of Cable Street of 1936, preventing Sir Oswald Mosley's British Union of Fascists from marching through London's East End. This period of popularity would continue until the outbreak of war in 1939, when the CPGB's initial hostility to a war against Soviet Russia's German allies again lost it many members and supporters. When in 1941 Germany invaded the Soviet Union, the CPGB immediately became one of the most vociferous proponents of war, opposing strike action and demanding that the Allies open a second front against Hitler. CPGB membership would peak at around 60,000 in 1943, and in the general election of 1945 Phil Piratin won London's Mile End constituency to join Gallacher in the House of Commons.

The post-war years saw a more fundamental shift in the CPGB as it adopted a new programme titled 'The British Road to Socialism', which committed the party to a peaceful, reformist transition to socialism. In the years that followed, the party would be at its most influential, both in the trade unions where many union officials were members, and among intellectuals. The Communist Party Historians Group was a particular focus of intellectual life, numbering Eric Hobsbawm, E P Thompson, Christopher Hill and John Saville among its more notable members.

CPGB membership went into decline after the Soviet Union crushed the Hungarian uprising of 1956, but the party remained strong in the trade union movement. Although communist control of the Electrical Trades Union was brought to an end by a ballot-rigging scandal that ended in a court case in 1959, the party enjoyed a number of successes, including the election of Hugh Scanlon to the presidency of the giant Amalgamated Engineering Union. The party was also little troubled by a split in world communism which forced communists to choose between Moscow and Peking. Here, just a handful of members initially left the CPGB in support of the Chinese communist position, to be followed later by a larger but still relatively insignificant group calling itself the Communist Party of Britain (Marxist-Leninist). The CPB(ML) would later subdivide still further when the communist governments of China and Albania went their separate ideological ways. A more significant blow to CPGB membership arose from the Soviet invasion of Czechoslovakia in 1968, and from the now socially conservative party's failure to capitalize on the student and youth protests of the same year.

By the mid-1970s, the CPGB was coming increasingly under the sway of 'Euro-communist' ideas, focused on cultural politics. Such an approach, which was open to feminism, gay rights and other social movements, tended to alienate the party's industrial militants who put class politics at the centre of their ideology. By the 1980s, the CPGB was tearing itself apart and the divide within the party had spawned a number of internal factions and breakaway parties. Following the collapse of the Soviet Union in 1991, the CPGB leadership, by now firmly in the hands of the Euro-communists, decided to close the party down and establish a think tank instead. This new body, Democratic Left, was succeeded in 1999 by the New Politics Network, which itself ceased to exist in 2007. A group of former CPGB members now operating as the Communist Party of Great Britain (Provisional Central Committee) claim to be the rightful successors to the old party.

Further research

The main archive of the Communist Party of Great Britain is held by the **Labour History Archive and Study Centre** in Manchester. Most administrative and political records before 1943 were sent to Moscow, and were deposited at the Marx-Lenin Institute, now the Russian Centre for Modern History. However, the archives contain microfilm of Comintern material relating to the CPGB in the 1920s and 1930s. The Labour History Archive also holds the archives of the London District Communist Party, including files on district congresses from 1926 onwards. A number of files remain closed to the public. An index to the collection can be searched through the Archives Hub at http://www.archiveshub.ac.uk/news/03122303.html.

The papers of the CPGB's long-serving general secretary Harry Pollitt are also in the Labour History Archive (see http://www.archiveshub.ac.uk/news/04031203.html).

Graham Stevenson, a trade union organizer and political activist, has been compiling a **Compendium of Communist Biography** which now runs to 700 entries and around 250,000 words and can be freely accessed at http://www.grahamstevenson.me.uk. He says on the site: 'No special objective has been applied to selecting names; rather they constitute a selection from a file of a large number of life stories garnered by myself over some decades from obituaries, biographies and memoirs. These were collected to satisfy my interest in the personalities of Party history and a wistful feeling that one day I would in some way help to retain their memories.'

The **CPGB Bibliography** at http://www.amielandmelburn.org.uk/cpgb_biblio/searchfrset.htm is the fruit of sixteen years of research in libraries, archives, basement rooms and garages – and lists thousands of books, pamphlets, magazines and articles, official papers and reports, academic theses and unpublished memoirs both by and about the Communist Party of Great Britain.

Less welcome attention came from the security services. A search of the **National Archives** catalogue (http://www.nationalarchives.gov.uk/catalogue) restricting results to the KV series and using only the word 'communist' reveals no fewer than 966 results, almost all of which are files opened by the security services on individuals who were known to be members or supporters of the CPGB, or were suspected – sometimes wrongly – of being so. Among those wrongly thought to be sympathetic to the CPGB were the writer George Orwell (see catalogue entry KV 2/2699).

The **National Archives** publishes a guide to security and intelligence history resources at http://www.nationalarchives.gov.uk/security history.

The **Socialist History Society** is the successor to the Communist Party History Group. It publishes the *Socialist History Journal* and a number of occasional papers can be downloaded from its website at http://www.socialisthistorysociety.co.uk. It is also developing an online archive of Communist Party History Group titles with the Barry Amiel and Norman Melburn Trust (see http://www.amieland melburn.org.uk).

Co-operative Party

Founded in October 1917 following a conference attended by more than 100 co-operative retail societies, the aim of the Central Co-operative Parliamentary Representation Committee, soon renamed the Co-operative Party, was to put co-operators into the House of Commons. It contested ten seats at the 1918 general election, and one candidate, Alfred Waterson, was successful in Kettering. The party went on to win local council seats, and raised its representation in Parliament to four in 1922, six in 1923 and five in 1924. Co-operative Party MPs took the Labour whip in Parliament from the start, and in 1927 the party entered into an electoral pact called the Cheltenham Agreement, under which the parties agreed not to oppose each other's candidates. In practice, this has meant that a certain number of candidates have stood at each election under a joint 'Labour and Co-operative Party' flag. The number of Labour and Co-operative MPs reached a peak of twenty-three after the general election of 1945 – a figure not equalled until Labour's 1997 landslide victory. The Co-operative Party has both individual members and affiliated members – local co-operative societies.

Further research

The Co-operative Party's records are held in the **National Co-operative Archive**, which also houses collections relating to the wider co-operative movement, from the Rochdale Pioneers onwards. There is an online guide to family history sources in the National Co-operative Archive at http://archive.co-op.ac.uk/downloadFiles/familyHistory Guide.pdf.

National Co-operative Archive, Co-operative College, Holyoake House, Hanover Street, Manchester M60 0AS
Tel: 0161 246 2925
Web: http://archive.co-op.ac.uk
A full list of all Labour and Co-operative Party MPs elected since 1918 can be found at http://en.wikipedia.org/wiki/List_of_Labour_Co-operative_Members_of_Parliament.

Common Wealth

Founded in July 1942, largely in protest at the wartime agreement between the major political parties not to fight each other at by-elections while hostilities continued, Common Wealth brought together members of the 1941 Committee, a think tank set up by Edward G Hulton, the owner of the *Picture Post* magazine, and dissident former Liberals led by Sir Richard Acland, who believed that their party had lost its sense of direction. Common Wealth developed a libertarian socialist stance which included an extension of common ownership, but not in the statist form advocated by the Labour Party and later implemented after 1945. The party's willingness to contest parliamentary by-elections in wartime proved successful, and by 1945 it had four MPs, including Acland himself, who won Barnstaple in 1942. The 1945 general election proved disastrous for Common Wealth. It lost all four seats, and was successful only in Chelmsford, where its candidate Ernest Millington took a seat that the Labour Party had failed to contest. At its annual conference in Hastings the following year, the party split, with the majority, including the party leadership and Millington, defecting to the Labour Party. The minority carried on until 1993, but gradually became a pressure group rather than a political party. The group played a part in the creation of the Industrial Common Ownership Movement which advocated workers' control of industries, and from the 1950s onwards was close to the Scottish, Welsh and Cornish nationalist movements.

Further research

Common Wealth's papers can be found in the **University of Sussex Library**. The collection includes minutes of national and branch meetings and the personal papers of Sir Richard Acland and Hugh Lawson, MP for Skipton, 1944–45, along with taped interviews by Angus Calder in 1964–65 with surviving members of the party. An index can be found on the Archives Hub website at http://www.archiveshub.ac.uk/news/0505commonwealth.html.

Socialist Party of Great Britain

Founded in 1904 by a group which broke with the Social Democratic Federation over its 'reformist' line and the increasingly erratic leadership of Henry Hyndman, the Socialist Party of Great Britain has barely shifted its political line in the 100-plus years since. Its approach is in a tradition known as 'impossibilism' which argues that reformism is of limited value in overturning capitalism and insists on revolutionary political action as the only reliable method of bringing about socialism. It differs from other impossibilist parties in its adherence to the ballot box as the means of achieving this revolution and has consistently rejected the Leninist ideas otherwise almost universally adopted within left-wing socialist parties after 1917. The SPGB had 104 members at its inaugural meeting and has since its launch published a magazine called the *Socialist Standard*. Membership

Members of the Socialist Party of Great Britain at their first annual conference in 1905. Copies of the photograph were subsequently sold for 2 shillings each to raise funds.

is still numbered only in the hundreds. Throughout its existence, the SPGB has refused to recognize common ground with any other party on the grounds that since it is the party of the working class, all others are, by definition, parties of the ruling class. Its opposition to wars as mere disputes within the capitalist class led many members to become conscientious objectors during the two world wars. The SPGB is also credited with developing the theory that the Soviet Union, far from being a socialist country, practised 'state capitalism'. In recent years, the SPGB has taken to calling itself The Socialist Party. It has a number of sister parties in the World Socialist Movement.

Further research

The SPGB has a website at http://www.worldsocialism.org/spgb which includes a series of articles published in the *Socialist Standard* since 1904.

The SPGB retains its own comprehensive archives. Access is by appointment only. Contact the Socialist Party of Great Britain, 52 Clapham High St, London SW4 7UN. Tel 020 7622 3811. Full details of the archive and its contents can be found at http://www.aim25.ac.uk/cgi-bin/search2?coll_id=7261&inst_id=96.

Papers collected by the historian and author Robert Barltrop, who was for many years a member of the SPGB, can be found in the **Bishopsgate Institute**. They include internal reports, conference papers and published works as well as photographs and sketches. The full catalogue is available at http://www.nationalarchives.gov.uk/a2a/records.aspx?cat=372-barltrop&cid=-1.

Robert Barltrop is also the author of *The Monument: The Story of the Socialist Party of Great Britain* (Pluto Press, 1976).

Trotskyism

When the founder of the Red Army, Leon Trotsky, was expelled from the Communist Party of the Soviet Union and forced into exile, he was not without his supporters in the wider communist movement. Here, his most enthusiastic supporters were to be found in the Communist Party of Great Britain's branches in suburban south London. Expelled from the CPGB after forming a loose grouping known as the Balham Group, these earliest Trotskyists formed the Communist League in 1932.

Rejecting Trotsky's advice to join the Independent Labour Party in order to 'transform it', the League opted instead to allow some of its members to form a secret revolutionary faction within the ILP. The move led to the first of the many splits which would later come to characterize the small but argumentative Trotskyist movement, with those inside the ILP forming a separate Marxist Group. By 1938 the remaining members of the Communist League had formed the Marxist League and started to organize within the Labour Party. In the same year, the Marxist Group and Marxist League came together to form the Revolutionary Socialist League.

Although this move united the main Trotskyist factions, a group calling itself the Workers International League refused to join, and during the next six years there would be a number of splits within the RSL, including factions known as the Revolutionary Workers League and the Socialist Workers League. By 1944, the RSL had been reduced from 300 to just twenty members, at which point a conference of the Fourth International (the international grouping of Trotskyist parties) forced it to merge with the WIL on its own terms to create the Revolutionary Communist Party.

Although membership numbers remained tiny, the main Trotskyist groupings had by now drawn in a number of key individuals who would continue to dominate ultra-left politics for decades to come: Ted Grant, later leader of the Militant entryist group within the Labour Party; Gerry Healy, whose Workers Revolutionary Party would eventually manage to publish its own daily newspaper with the help of some very rich backers; and Tony Cliff, whose Socialist Workers Party's placards became an unavoidable fixture on almost every protest march and picket line from the late 1970s onwards.

Further research

Although there have been large numbers of parties, groups, factions and tendencies claiming allegiance to Trotskyism over the past three-quarters of a century, very few of these organizations have left official collections of their archives. In part this can be attributed to the secrecy with which some groups have surrounded themselves, and in part to the often short-lived nature of the groups.

The most comprehensive collections relating to Trotskyism in Britain can be found in the **Modern Records Centre at Warwick University**. Among the papers to be found here are:

• papers of the International Marxist Group from 1964 onwards, and those of IMG members including Richard Hyman, Steve Jefferys, Richard Kuper, Alistair Mutch and Stirling Smith;

• papers of the Spartacist League, a tiny faction which operated mainly in London after 1975;

• personal archives collected by Jimmy Deane, Ken Tarbuck and Denzil Dean Harber, all of whom played an active part in Trotskyist groups from the early 1930s onwards;

• personal papers of Tony Cliff, the leading figure in the Socialist Workers Party until his death in 2002.

The **Labour History Archive and Study Centre** in Manchester holds records on Trotskyist groups and individuals collected by the Communist Party of Great Britain.

Chapter 9

THE LABOUR MOVEMENT AT PRAYER AND PLAY

Little remains today of the network of social activities that defined the labour movement from the 1890s to the Second World War. But for those who wanted it, and there were thousands who did, there was once an astonishing array of institutions offering almost an entire alternative lifestyle – ranging from cycling clubs to holiday camps, Sunday schools to churches, book clubs to theatres.

Inevitably, few records have survived from many of these organizations. But it is still possible to piece together something of their history from the black-and-white postcards, secular hymn books and leaflets that remain. Much of what we know about these organizations comes from newspaper reports of the time. And surprisingly, at least one of these late Victorian socialist institutions – the National Clarion Cycling Club – is still thriving.

Socialist Sunday Schools

For a generation of left-wing parents, Socialist Sunday Schools offered a secular alternative to the educational top-ups offered by church and chapel. For the children who sang the movement's religion-free hymns and studied working-class history, it provided an introduction to an alternative cultural tradition and a very different set of values to that found in the schools of the period.

The first Socialist Sunday School was established in 1892 in Battersea, South London, by Mary Gray, a member of the Social Democratic Federation who had been shocked at how little education was available to the children of the men and women she worked with during the Great Dock Strike of 1889. Two years later, a similar school was established in Glasgow by the SDF activist and trade unionist Tom Anderson with Caroline Martyn and Archie McArthur. From these small beginnings, there quickly arose a substantial movement.

By 1896 there were sixteen Socialist Sunday Schools, the best documented of which were those founded in Salford that same year. Both were started by local branches of the Social Democratic Federation and one met in the SDF's own clubhouse at 43 Trafford Road. A third school opened in 1899, coming under the wing of the socialist feminist Sylvia Pankhurst, who decorated it in the style of William Morris. On New Year's Day, 300 children were entertained there at a sit-down tea.

Within twenty years of the first Socialist Sunday School, there was a National Council of British Socialist Sunday Schools (founded in 1909), a newspaper called *The Young Socialist* (first published in 1901) and no fewer than 120 schools throughout the country, many of them with student rolls running into hundreds.

The schools had not just their own hymns but their own hymn books, specimen lessons approved by the national council, a naming ceremony inherited from the Chartist and Owenite schools of a half century earlier, and a socialist 'ten commandments'. These ranged from the first commandment:

Love your schoolfellows, who will be your fellow workmen in life

through to a seventh which enjoined children to

Remember that all good things of the earth are produced by labour. Whoever enjoys them without working for them is stealing the bread of the workers

and a tenth, urging

Look forward to the day when all men and women will be free citizens of one fatherland and live together as brothers and sisters in peace and righteousness.

Socialist Sunday Schools provided a valuable addition to the very basic education then on offer to children in their day schools, but constantly ran up against difficulties, especially in finding suitable homes. In 1907, the London County Council evicted five branches from hired school buildings, and many schools had no option but to use Labour halls. However, it was the outbreak of war in 1914 which provided the greatest challenge to the schools' continued existence as many teachers were either called up or were imprisoned as conscientious objectors.

After the war, with the Social Democratic Federation now

transformed into the Communist Party of Great Britain, the labour movement's previous unity began to fracture, with the children of communists often directed into the Young Pioneers instead. In 1931 the Labour Party and Independent Labour Party also moved in separate directions, resulting in the former refusing permission for the latter to use its premises. By 1939, the movement was effectively finished.

Further research

The Working Class Movement Library in Salford holds a selection of Socialist Sunday School hymn, tune and song books along with a number of pamphlets and leaflets. It also holds runs of *The Young Socialist* which contain much information about the schools' activities. Records of the Halifax Socialist Sunday School are held by the West Yorkshire Archive Service (http://www.archives.wyjs.org.uk).

Labour Churches

While Socialist Sunday Schools were largely secular, the Labour Church had its roots in the Christian Socialist movement founded in the late 1840s and which had proved influential in the political development of many Independent Labour Party figures, including James Keir Hardie, the future Labour Chancellor of the Exchequer Philip Snowden, and the dockers' union leader Ben Tillett.

A page from the Labour Church tune book. Source: author's collection.

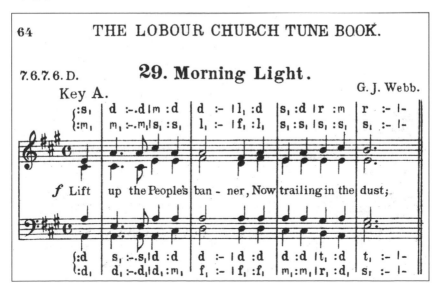

The first Labour Church was established in October 1891 by John Trevor, who had resigned as a Unitarian minister to establish his own chapel in Manchester, in the belief that the labour movement could be the means of obtaining 'the kingdom of god on earth'. Its first service, in Chorlton Town Hall, was opened by a string band, after which Trevor led the prayers, there was a reading from the work of the romantic poet James Russell Lowell, and a Unitarian minister read the lesson before the choir sang Edward Carpenter's socialist hymn 'England Arise'. Its second service a week later heard from Robert Blatchford, founder and editor of *The Clarion* newspaper.

Other churches soon followed. In 1892, a Bradford Labour Church was set up after the local Unitarian minister upset his congregation by supporting the Liberal candidate against the socialist Ben Tillett in that year's general election, and by 1895 there were at least fifty Labour Churches. Many of these were involved in charity work, running homeless shelters and schools, and attempting to alleviate slum conditions.

In 1892, Trevor had also begun publication of *The Labour Prophet*, a monthly magazine which ran for six years. There was also a Labour Church Union, founded in 1893, which sought to raise funds for the movement. In the same year, more than 5,000 people attended a service to mark the foundation of the Independent Labour Party at a conference in Bradford, and at its peak the movement could claim twenty-five affiliated churches. In all, as many as 120 such churches may have existed at one time or another.

However, the Labour Church's aims were never particularly clear and Trevor was unhappy with the leadership role expected of him. Trevor was particularly unhappy with the lack of prominence given by other leading figures in the movement to its spiritual dimension. By 1900, he was no longer playing a prominent role in the increasingly secular Labour Church. His son, Stanley Trevor, would later recall: 'My father once told me he lost interest in the Labour Church largely because it tended to become merely a Sunday meeting of Trade Unionists and so lost its religious character.'

Without Trevor, the Labour Church movement went into a rapid decline. Although there was a brief resurgence of interest after the ILP's successes in the 1906 general election, this was short-lived and only one or two churches survived the First World War.

Further research

There are few surviving records of the Labour Churches; however, the **Labour History Archive and Study Centre** holds a number of papers, including invitations to speakers. A list of these holdings can be found using the Access to Archives service at http://www.nationalarchives.gov.uk/a2a.

The **London School of Economics** also holds some Labour Church pamphlets, some of which are listed at http://www.lse.ac.uk/library/Default.htm.

There is a Labour Church file at **Warwick University's Modern Records Centre** consisting of handbills, hymn sheets and reports from 1891 to 1910, as well as working papers on John Trevor compiled by the Rev. G W Brassington for an unpublished life of Trevor.

An entry for John Trevor can be found in volume six of *The Dictionary of Labour Biography* (Macmillan, 1982).

Socialist Holiday Camps

One of the first holiday camps established in the UK was set up by John Fletcher Dodd, an ardent socialist, vegetarian and cyclist, who in 1906 opened the Caister Socialist Holiday Camp near Great Yarmouth on the Norfolk coast. Dodd had been a founder member of the Independent Labour Party, and his aim was to give socialist and trade unionist friends from the East End the chance to get some fresh air away from the London grime.

The camp was literally that to start with – guests stayed under canvas. It was also initially an all-male affair, though that changed in 1909. Dodd ran the camp his own way: there was a ban on alcohol, gambling and bad language. Guests were expected to be quiet after 11 pm, each day began with a bracing exercise routine, and there were lectures on a Sunday. The cost was one guinea – around a week's wages.

After the First World War, the camp became more permanent, with chalets in place of tents. Later, when in 1933 Great Yarmouth withdrew its tram service, Dodd bought twenty-two of the tram bodies and converted them for use as accommodation. The camp proved popular with senior Labour figures, and George Bernard Shaw, Keir Hardie and Herbert Morrison all stayed at one time. Although forced to close during the Second World War, the camp reopened in 1946. By this time, there were few political elements to a holiday at Caister and, following

Dodd's death at the age of 90 in 1952, Miss Caister and knobbly knees competitions were introduced.

The camp remains in operation today, having spawned an entire holiday industry. One early guest was a South African by the name of Billy Butlin. But the camp's political heritage has not been entirely lost. Inspired by the Caister experiment, in the 1930s the local government union NALGO opened its own holiday centres at Croyd Bay in Devon and at Cayton Bay, Scarborough. Now operated by NALGO's successor union, Unison, the Croyd Bay Holiday Village remains in operation today.

Further research

The BBC marked the centenary of the Caister camp in 2006. Information and a film clip can be found on the BBC website. Go to http://www.bbc.co.uk and search on the term 'Inside out: 100 years of holiday fun'. The Seaside History website at http://www.seaside history.co.uk/camps.html also has an account of the camp's development.

The Clarion Movement

Launched by the idiosyncratic journalist Robert Blatchford in 1891, *The Clarion* was just one of many such newspapers vying for readers in the late Victorian labour movement. But working out of a tiny office in Corporation Street, Manchester, the penny paper's small editorial staff created a phenomenon which would be the envy of any modern publisher. In its early days, the paper enjoyed a circulation of 30,000 to 40,000 a week – a healthy but by no means spectacular number. But Blatchford's paper did more than inform its readers; it inspired them to engage with it and to spread the *Clarion* word far and wide, and by 1908 it could claim 80,000 sales every week.

Following the invention of the safety bicycle in the 1880s, the following decade saw cycling become something of a craze. Bicycles were, relatively, cheap to buy and almost free to run. They gave people a mobility they had not previously known, allowing working men and a few brave women to venture out into the countryside. And most of all, they made it possible for socialists to combine their politics with a healthy and enjoyable hobby. The first Clarion Cycling Club was launched at a meeting at Birmingham Labour Church in February 1894 – just in time for its seven members to enjoy a two-day Easter tour of

Postcard showing a debate between readers of The Clarion *and the Independent Labour Party's* Labour Leader. *They would take opposing sides in supporting and opposing the First World War.* Source: author's collection.

Worcestershire. By the end of the year there were clubs in Hanley, Liverpool, Bradford and Barnsley, and at Easter 1895 the National Clarion Club was founded and held its first annual conference.

From the start, the Clarion Cyclists combined their tours with political 'missionary' work. Every weekend while the weather permitted, Clarion Scouts set out from their urban bases to sell copies of *The Clarion* and Blatchford's *Merrie England* pamphlet in surrounding villages. Scouting groups were also encouraged to hold meetings and try to set up branches of the Independent Labour Party or Social Democratic Federation as they went along. Their efforts were not always appreciated, however, and on more than one occasion Clarion missionaries were moved on by the police or even arrested for causing an obstruction.

The Clarion also inspired its readers to other activities. In 1896, Julia Dawson, a reader of the paper, announced plans for a Clarion Women's Van, which would tour market towns and villages for thirteen weeks of the summer, holding open air meetings and spreading the socialist word. That summer, the van set off from Chester, visiting Bridgenorth,

Newcastle-under-Lyme, Macclesfield and Stockport, holding meetings that often attracted crowds of up to 500 people. Further tours, and a second van, followed in subsequent years, and the women's van continue to operate until the summer of 1914, taking *The Clarion* message to thousands of men and women.

The Clarion movement did not stop there. With the cycling clubs well established, members found a need for clubhouses where they could meet and socialize. There were annual Clarion camps. For the musically inclined there were Clarion Vocal Unions. Clarion Players and Dramatic Societies grew up. There were Clarion Field Clubs and Rambling Societies, Clarion Camera Clubs, Clarion Handicraft Guilds – and for those with no particular hobby, a Clarion Fellowship which simply provided an opportunity for socialists to meet each other socially.

Politically, however, all was not well. Blatchford alienated many *Clarion* readers through his support of the Boer War, and his subsequent anti-German views and jingoism at the outbreak of the First World War effectively cut his paper's ties to the mainstream of the labour movement. Many of the Clarion clubs ceased to exist during or after the war, and the paper itself struggled on in much reduced form until 1934 before ceasing publication. But the Clarion Cycling Club thrived, and enjoyed a second golden period in the 1920s and 1930s. Astonishingly, the Club is still going today – and though effectively now an apolitical body purely interested in cycling, it still carries the Clarion name and remains proud of its heritage.

Further research

The **National Clarion Cycling Club** maintains a website about its current cycling activities at http://www.clarioncc.org. The main archive collection is held in Manchester:
Manchester Archives & Local Studies, Central Library, St Peter's Square, Manchester M2 5PD
Tel: 0161 234 1959
Web: http://www.manchester.gov.uk/libraries/arls
Records of individual Clarion clubs are best located using the Access to Archives search on the National Archives website at http://www.nationalarchives.gov.uk/a2a.
Fellowship is Life: The National Cycling Clarion Club 1895–1995 by Denis Pye (Clarion Publishing, 1995) looks beyond the club's cycling

activities to talk about many of the Clarion movement's political and social activities. There is also a short account based on information in the book on the Working Class Movement Library website at http://www.wcml.org.uk/contents/creativity-and-culture/leisure.

The British Library Newspaper Library holds a complete run of *The Clarion* on microfilm at its Colindale site.

At the time of writing, the British Library is winding down the Colindale site with a view to moving all newspapers to Boston Spa in Yorkshire in 2011. Access to digital and microfilm copies of newspapers will be available at the British Library's reading rooms at St Pancras. See http://www.bl.uk/news/2007/pressrelease20070301.html for further information.

The Left Book Club

Founded in 1936 by the publisher Victor Gollancz, the Left Book Club numbered 57,000 members and supported around 1,500 discussion groups by the outbreak of the Second World War. Club members received a book of the month, chosen by Gollancz, the economist and political scientist Harold Laski, and the Communist (and later Labour) MP John Strachey.

The books had distinctive red and orange covers and sold for 2s. 6d. to members. Many were available only in the LBC edition, and there were additional optional titles reprinting socialist classics. The volumes included history, science, fiction and reportage, and among the authors were Arthur Koestler, Andréw Malraux, George Orwell and Clement Attlee.

In its early days, the club was reluctant to publish any criticism of the Soviet Union, and refused to publish Orwell's account of his experiences fighting in the Spanish Civil War, *Homage to Catalonia*. Some of the titles it did publish were little more than apologias for Stalinism. But after 1941, when Gollancz broke with the Communist Party of Great Britain, the club took a democratic socialist turn.

Despite its popularity the Left Book Club was never profitable, and when paper was rationed on the outbreak of war it was restricted to one title a month. Gollancz made up for this with a series of shorter monographs, including *Guilty Men* by Cato – a polemic in which the Labour MP Michael Foot laid the blame for Britain's wartime predicament at the door of the Conservative appeasers.

Further research

The papers of Sir Victor Gollancz are held at the **Modern Records Centre** at **Warwick University**. They relate mainly to his personal humanitarian and political interests but include some material on the Left Book Club.

The Working Class Movement Library holds an extensive but incomplete collection of Left Book Club titles, which are listed at http://www.wcml.org.uk/culture/lbcbooks.htm.

There is a further run of Left Book Club titles and microfilmed copies of the club's Left News newsletter in the special collections at **Sheffield University**. Further information on this collection is available at http://www.shef.ac.uk/library/libdocs/leftbook.pdf.

Unity Theatres

UNITY THEATRE SCHOOL

Approved by the L.C.C., the Joint Education Committee of the London Co-operative Societies, and the Left Book Club Theatre Guild. The only School for the progressive theatre movement.

COURSES OF HIGHEST
PROFESSIONAL STANDARD

in

PRODUCTION
ACTING
PLAYWRITING
STAGE-
MANAGEMENT

Under highly qualified tutors, including people who have helped to make UNITY THEATRE famous, assisted by leading figures in the Theatre World such as

Sybil Thorndyke
Lionel Britton
Maurice Browne
Lewis Casson
John Fernald
S. I. Hsiung
Miles Malleson
Herbert Marshall
Paul Robeson
Flora Robson
Alan Bush, L.R.A.M.
Michel St. Denis
Andre van Gyseghem
etc.

UNDER THE ARTISTIC DIRECTION
of
HERBERT MARSHALL
Unity Theatre Producer

Principal for the L.C.C.:
EDWIN C. WHITE

FEES: 15/- per course per ann.

There had been numerous sporadic attempts to create socialist or workers' theatres, and as early as 1912 the National Association of Clarion Dramatic Clubs established the People's Theatre in Newcastle. Both the Independent Labour Party and the Communist Party also operated local amateur theatrical clubs for their members. However, from 1926 to 1935 it was the Communist Party which took the lead in co-ordinating a national Workers' Theatre movement as an explicit propaganda tool, staging plays with a socialist and revolutionary theme. Other left-wing groups included the Red Megaphones in Salford and Hackney People's Players.

The Unity Theatre, established in 1936, grew out of these movements, but had a permanent base initially in an old church hall in Britannia Street, King's Cross, and subsequently in Goldington Street, Camden. Unity Theatre was organized as a co-operative society, with each member paying one shilling to join, and receiving a share number that had to be stated when booking seats. The annual

Advert for the Unity Theatre School from the theatre's programme for its production of 'Babes in the Wood – a Pantomime with Political Point'. Source: author's collection.

subscription was a further shilling. Unity Theatre and its associated local groups worked closely with the Left Book Club Theatre Guild. By 1939 there were 250 theatre groups and plans for a training school for actors, producers and technicians. After the war the remaining fifty branches became more closely organized into the Unity Theatre Society Limited, which was largely amateur. Local branches of Unity Theatres provided venues for left-wing theatre. But by the 1960s the movement was in decline as the abolition of licensing meant that mainstream theatres could more readily meet the demand for radical productions. Although the original theatre burned down in the 1970s, a Unity Theatre Trust remains in operation.

Further research

The main Unity Theatre collection is in the **Labour History Archive and Study Centre** in Manchester. It includes scripts, press cuttings, minutes, festival programmes, correspondence and financial statements from the 1930s onwards, but most material dates from the 1960s.

Papers from the Bristol Unity Players Club can be found at **Warwick University's Modern Records Centre**. They include: minutes, 1937–46; correspondence, 1938–47; scripts; programmes; photographs. The Communist Party of Great Britain published a pamphlet in its Our History series on the Bristol Players: *The People's Theatre in Bristol 1930–45*, by A Tuckett (CPGB, 1979).

The records of the Glasgow Unity Theatre are in **Glasgow University Library**'s special collections department and run from 1941 to 1967: Hillhead Street, Glasgow G12 8QE
Tel: 0141 330 6767
Web: http://special.lib.gla.ac.uk

A list of material held in the Unity Theatre Trust archives can be seen at http://www.unitytheatre.org.uk.

Workers Sports' Clubs

The British Workers' Sport Federation was established in 1923 by Clarion Cyclists, Labour Party sympathizers and trade union officials. Its goal was international unity and peace through sport. But unable to tolerate the increasing dominance of the organization by the Communist Party, Labour Party members and trade unionists left the organization in 1930 and formed the British Workers' Sports Association.

In 1931 the BWSA sent a small team to the second Workers' Olympiad in Vienna and came fourth out of twenty-one teams. Although the political divide between the Labour and Communist parties made international competition difficult, teams continued to be fielded at successive workers' events until the Second World War. The BWSA was wound up in 1960.

The BWSF survived the loss of its Labour and trade unionist members, and in 1932 its members were at the forefront of the Kinder Scout mass trespass movement to open up the Peak District to walkers. Both the BWSA and BWSF campaigned for the state to regulate and provided resources for sports.

Further research

Papers relating to both the BWSF and BWSA are held at the **Labour History Archive and Study Centre in Manchester**.

An article by Stephen G Jones, 'Sport, politics and the labour movement: the British workers' sports federation, 1923–1935' appeared in the *International Journal of the History of Sport*, vol. 2, issue 2 (1985).

Chapter 10

ELECTIONS AND THE FRANCHISE

By the beginning of the nineteenth century, the population of Great Britain (excluding Ireland) had grown to just under 11 million. The number of those entitled to vote, however, was tiny and most certainly did not include the sort of working men who would later come together in the trade union and labour movement – let alone women.

The story of Britain's emerging parliamentary democracy traditionally begins with the Reform Act of 1832. Yet even this Act (more properly the Representation of the People Act 1832) managed only to nudge the size of the electorate up from some 400,000 to around 650,000 in a population which now numbered 16.5 million men and women. The Act also shook up parliamentary constituencies and for the first time gave representation to some of the great new industrial centres of the North and Midlands. But perhaps more important from the perspective of family historians, it introduced electoral registration.

Introducing the Electoral Register

The electoral register, as it is most commonly known, is more properly called the Register of Electors. Other names include the electoral roll or electoral list, voters' register, voters' roll or voters' list. The electors' list, or list of electors, is not the same thing. It is a provisional list of voters produced ahead of the main register so that entries can be checked for accuracy.

Almost every year since 1832 has seen the publication of a new electoral register. However, there were no new registers in 1916 or 1917 because of the First World War, and publication was again suspended from 1940–44 inclusive. There were two registers each year from 1919–26 and again from 1945–46. Constituency boundaries were revised in 1868 and 1885, so there were two registers in each of those years, the second of which lasted until the end of the following year.

Pages from the electoral register. This register, from 1945, lists men and women voters on war service. Photograph: Simon Fowler.

Electoral registers have always contained as a minimum the first name and surname of each person qualified to vote, along with their 'place of abode'. Unfortunately, this does not always mean a full address. Until 1948, registers also set out the qualification which entitled each person to the vote, and some include additional information, such as an elector's qualification for jury service or their status as an absent voter.

After 1918, with many men still away from home on military service, many electors were listed as absent voters, enabling them to vote by post or by proxy. Sometimes, such entries will include service numbers and regimental details, opening up new avenues of research.

An ancestor's qualification for the vote will provide a key piece of information. Interpreting it, however, requires some understanding of how the franchise has grown over the years, and the different qualifications in force at different times.

Extending the Franchise

Parliamentary elections

Before 1832, the qualifications required to vote varied from constituency to constituency. Since the Representation of the People Act 1832, the franchise has been increasingly widened and standardized. By 1918, the vote had been extended to almost all men and to many women, and this disparity was itself abolished in 1928 when women won the vote on the same basis as men.

Although the earliest legislation mentioned here was for England and Wales, separate but similar Acts were passed for Scotland and Ireland in both 1832 and 1867. The main Acts of Parliament affecting the franchise – and consequently whose names appear on each year's electoral register – were:

Representation of the People Act 1832 – Allows all men over 21 meeting property qualifications to vote. In counties, the vote went to 40 shilling freeholders, owners of land in copyhold worth £10, holders of long-term leases on land worth £10, holders of medium-term leases on land worth £50, and tenants-at-will paying annual rent of £50. In the boroughs, the vote was given to all men who owned or leased land

A medallion issued to mark the successful passage of the Reform Act of 1832. It celebrates on the front Earl Grey and other 'zealous and successful promoters of reform', and on the reverse proclaims, 'The purity of the constitution restored'.
Source: author's collection.

worth £10, except in the freeman boroughs where the right to vote was restricted to those with the 'freedom of the borough'.

Representation of the People Act 1867 – Adds 1.5 million men to the electoral register by giving the vote to adult male urban householders and male lodgers paying £10 a year for unfurnished rooms.

Representation of the People Act 1884 – Extends the voting qualifications introduced for boroughs in 1867 to rural, county areas, taking the electorate to more than 5.5 million.

Representation of the People Act 1918 – Gives the vote to practically all men over 21 and to women over 30, taking the size of the electorate to more than 21 million.

Representation of the People Act 1948 – Abolishes plural voting which allowed anyone who lived in one constituency but owned property in another to vote in both places, and which permitted graduates of Oxford and Cambridge universities to elect a second, university MP.

Representation of the People Act 1969 – Lowers the voting age from 21 to 18.

POLL BOOKS

While electoral registers list those entitled to vote, poll books recorded the names and political affiliations of those who actually cast their votes.

Before the introduction of the secret ballot in 1872, electors were required to state publicly how they wished to cast their votes, raising concerns about the influence of landlords and employers over the new working-class voters. This meant a public record could be maintained by local political organizers in order to provide a head start on electoral canvassing at future elections.

Some of these have survived to be republished by family history groups and local record societies. For example, family history publishers such as S&N Genealogy (http://www.genealogysupplies.com/index.htm) are able to supply some poll books on CD-rom.

The largest collection of original poll books is at the Institute of Historical Research in London, while the locations of surviving poll books are given in Jeremy Gibson and Colin Rogers' *Poll Books* (4th edition, Family History Partnership, 2008).

Among the poll books available free online are those for:
• Liverpool in 1832 at http://www.liverpool-genealogy.org.uk/1832Pollbook/Pollbook1832.htm
• Dorset in 1807 at http://www.thedorsetpage.com/genealogy/info/poll_book.htm
• Nottingham in 1785 at http://www.charliespage.co.uk/pollbook index.htm

Dr John Dawson of Abacus Genealogy Research has published a Bedfordshire poll book of 1784 online at http://www.rabancourt.co.uk/abacus/p1784h.html along with a helpful discussion of the possible pitfalls in using such resources.

Women and the vote

Although it was generally assumed that all electors were men, it was not until the 1832 Act that this was specifically set out in law. The first women would not appear on electoral registers until 1869, when the Municipal Franchise Act gave women ratepayers the right to vote in some local elections and serve as poor law guardians.

In practice, very few women were able to vote under this Act until later reforms to married women's property rights were carried through. From this date, however, women gradually began to appear on the register, especially after 1888 when they also won the right to vote in county and borough council elections.

Women would not win the right to vote in parliamentary elections until 1918, when the franchise was extended to women over the age of 30 who were householders, the wives of householders, who occupied property with an annual rent of £5 or were university graduates. It would be another ten years before the Representation of the People Act 1928 gave women the vote on the same basis as men at the age of 21.

Local elections

Local government was in a shambolic state in the early part of the nineteenth century. It had failed to adapt to the growth of towns and cities, and in some boroughs the ruling corporations were self-selected and self-perpetuating oligarchies. The Municipal Corporations Act

1835 began the process of cleaning up local corruption and bringing democracy to local government.

For the first time town councils were required to subject themselves to election by ratepayers – a rather wider franchise than that for parliamentary elections. This meant that each borough needed to compile a burgess roll – in effect a list of ratepayers – for use as a local election register. By 1869, the first women had begun to appear on these local registers.

Separate electoral registers for parliamentary and local elections were maintained until 1878, when local authorities were allowed and later ordered to merge the two. Burgess rolls will almost always contain more names than parliamentary registers because the franchise was wider, but because there was less variety in the qualifications to vote at local level they may also be less revealing.

The wider electoral franchise to be found in local government did mean that labour representatives succeeded in winning public office earlier at this level than in the House of Commons. As early as 1842, Chartist candidates succeeded in winning election in Leeds to the town improvement commission. They would continue to hold office on the town council when it was established, and from the 1850s formed the core of the Liberal group on the council.

The election of working men and women as poor law guardians from the 1880s made a significant difference to the running of the workhouse system. One of the most prominent of these was Will Crooks, who as a child experienced at first hand the horrors of workhouse life and schooling, and who later sat alongside George Lansbury as one of two labour representatives on the Poplar Board of Guardians. Within five years, Crooks had become chairman of the board, turning Poplar into a model authority which dramatically improved the diet of workhouse inmates, abolished their humiliatingly distinctive uniforms, and introduced proper schooling for their children.

Excluded from the Vote

Throughout the nineteenth century and well into the twentieth, there was a long and ever-shifting list of categories of people excluded from the vote and therefore likely to be missing from electoral registers. Although many of these groups were specifically excluded by legislation, others were disenfranchised when their right to vote was challenged in the courts.

One legal text on the subject published in 1852 cites three reasons why individuals who otherwise met the property qualifications of the time would be excluded from voting: want of intelligence, want of integrity, and want of independence.

Into the first category came anyone classed as an 'idiot' – defined as 'destitute of understanding from his birth, and never has lucid intervals'. Into the second came anyone convicted of a felony (a serious crime), perjury or of personating a voter. But it is the third category which is the most diverse. Among those thought to lack sufficient independence to vote were, most notably, women. In 1852, their exclusion appeared so obviously natural that a tiny number of historical cases of women voting as far back as Tudor times could be dismissed as 'curious instances' by the author of a specialist legal text for lawyers and judges.

Others felt to lack sufficient independence (usually from the authorities responsible for overseeing elections) to be entitled to vote included:

• town clerks, because of their paid role as clerks to the returning officer;
• police officers, who did not get a vote in parliamentary elections until the Police Disabilities Removal Act 1877 and who had to wait until 1893 to vote in local elections;
• postmasters, letter carriers and even the servants of the postmaster;
• those receiving parish relief – in effect, a disqualification from voting on the grounds of extreme poverty – until 1893 in local elections and 1918 in parliamentary elections.

In addition to these groups, peers of the realm had no vote and no right to be on the electoral register because they were represented in the Lords rather than the Commons. Finally, aliens, even when naturalized as British subjects, were excluded from voting on the grounds that their allegiances might lie elsewhere.

This list would vary over time to include or exclude certain groups. Somewhat vindictively, after the First World War, conscientious objectors were disenfranchised for five years from 1918 until they regained the vote in 1923. The practice was not repeated after the Second World War.

1911: A SNAPSHOT OF THE ELECTORATE

By the end of the Edwardian era, the majority of men had the vote in parliamentary elections, though women still did not.

The electorate had grown since the most recent, 1884, reform act, because both the adult population itself and the number of those meeting the qualification had increased. Figures drawn from parliamentary papers of the time* show there to be 7,904,000 electors. However, this does not mean that there were as many individual voters, as some half a million men were registered more than once, and could vote in two or even more constituencies.

To be on the register, men had to meet one or more of the property qualifications still in place. Official figures show that the nearly 8 million votes could be claimed for these reasons:

Householders – owners or tenants of any land or tenement of £10 annual value – 84.3 per cent

Lodgers – those renting rooms valued unfurnished at £10 a year – 4.6 per cent

Property – 40 shilling freeholders and other freeholders, copyholders and leaseholders (almost wholly in the rural counties) – 8.4 per cent

Service – inhabitant occupiers of a separate dwelling house through their employment or office, not as owner or tenant – 1.8 per cent

University graduates – 0.6 per cent

Freemen – freemen by birth or apprenticeship in boroughs where the qualification had existed before 1832 – 0.3 per cent.

* Cited in *The Making of Modern British Politics*, by Martin Pugh (Blackwell Publishing, 2002).

Using Electoral Registers

Some problems

For all their fascination, electoral registers are not always easy to navigate. Until 1918, electoral registers compiled for parliamentary elections were mostly in alphabetical order of elector by parish. Local burgess rolls, on the other hand, reflected the practice of collecting rates from door to door and were usually ordered by streets.

Over time, it became common practice to organize all registers in street order, making it hard to track down an individual whose address cannot be narrowed to a relatively small geographical area. This may require some preliminary work with other local directories.

Since parliamentary and local government boundaries often do not coincide, it can also be a frustrating job to track down the correct register – and street indexes compiled by local authorities may cover only part of a constituency, or there may be two registers. Where one local authority area includes two or more constituencies, there may be only one index which lists all streets indiscriminately without distinguishing between constituencies.

Finally, data protection concerns mean that more recent registers can be consulted only under strict rules which prevent the copying and re-use of information, and as a result some archives restrict access to them.

Despite these problems, electoral registers can help to flesh out the details of our ancestors' lives. In addition to being able to see them gain the vote for the first time as the franchise was extended, we may be able to find out what property they owned, or understand their status as householder or lodger.

Finding electoral registers

The greatest single collection of electoral registers is held by the British Library, which has around 20,000 registers from the period 1832–1931. Even this, however, is far from being a complete set. An online guide published by the Library describes the collection as 'modest to 1885, good from then until 1915 and modest again from 1918 to 1931'.

Surprisingly, it then has very few registers for the 1930s or for the first half of the 1940s. From 1947 onwards, however, it has a complete set of registers, including the full but not the edited versions published after 2002. A full list of the registers held at the British Library can be found in *Parliamentary Constituencies and Their Registers Since 1832*, which is available to visitors to the library.

The British Library also publishes an excellent guide to UK electoral registers and their uses online at http://www.bl.uk/reshelp/ findhelprestype/offpubs/electreg/electoralregisters.pdf, and has an online electoral register search service. It will check one address in one pre-2001 register and supply a copy of the entry. It charges £39 for this service. Further information and an online order form are available at http://www.bl.uk/reshelp/atyourdesk/docsupply/productsservices /researchservice/products/familyhistory. (Or go to http://www.bl. uk/reshelp/index.html and search on the term 'electoral registers'.)

Despite the impressive scale of the British Library collection, family historians are likely to find a visit to the relevant local records office or local studies library more fruitful. The National Archives also holds a small collection from the 1870s. Local records offices often hold more complete records for a specific area, and researchers can benefit from the expert local advice of their staff, along with finding aids such as street and trade directories and maps.

Both the Archon Directory of record repositories (http://www. nationalarchives.gov.uk/archon) and the Familia directory of family history resources in public libraries (http://www.familia.org.uk) can help you find the records office you need. There is a list of local records offices and links to their websites on the Mytimemachine website at http://www.mytimemachine.co.uk/archives.htm.

Further Reading

Electoral Registers and Burgess Rolls 1832–1948, by Jeremy Gibson (Family History Partnership, 2008) lists the location of all surviving electoral rolls.

Electoral Franchise: Who Can Vote? is a House of Commons library research note explaining who currently can and cannot vote in the UK. It is available at http://www.parliament.uk/commons/lib/research/ notes/snpc-02208.pdf.

A manual of the parliamentary election law of the United Kingdom of Great Britain and Ireland, by Samuel Warren, was published in 1852 by the legal publisher Butterworths. Among other things, it explains who could and could not vote at the mid-point of the nineteenth century and the reasons why. It can be found at http://books.google.com/ books?id=y7EDAAAAQAAJ&dq.

The reader-generated Wikipedia has information on many of the Acts of Parliament which extended and rationalized the franchise from 1832 onwards. Begin at http://en.wikipedia.org/wiki/ Representation_ of_the_People_Act.

Appendix 1

THE RISE AND FALL OF TRADE UNION MEMBERSHIP

The rise and fall of trade union membership 1900–2008

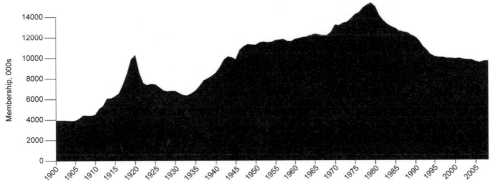

Trade union membership has plummeted since its peak of more than 13 million, but as the chart shows, it remains two and a half times higher today than it was at the turn of the twentieth century.

How the number of trade unions declined 1900–2008

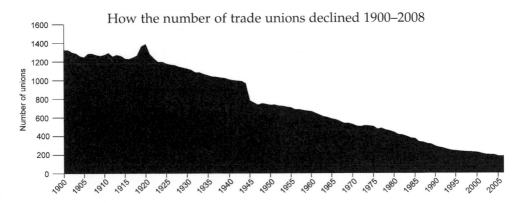

The number of trade unions has fallen rapidly and regardless of whether union membership was rising or falling. Sources for data: Registrar of Friendly Societies and Certification Officer annual reports.

CHRONOLOGY OF THE LABOUR MOVEMENT

1799
and
1800   Combination Acts: virtually all trade union activity illegal and subject to three months' imprisonment by the Justices of the Peace

1819   First Factory Act stops children under nine from working in factories and limits those aged nine to sixteen to 72 hours

1824   Combination Acts repealed; Steam Engine Makers' Society formed

1825   New Combination Act restricts union activities

1826   Journeymen Steam Engine and Machine Makers' Friendly Society formed

1831   Friendly Society of Operative Stone Masons of England, Ireland and Wales and United Operative Masons' Association of Scotland founded

1832   Great Reform Act abolishes rotten boroughs and establishes standard franchise

1833   Grand National Consolidated Trades Union formed

1834   Trial of 'Tolpuddle Martyrs' followed by transportation to Australia; Tobacco Workers' Union begins life as Friendly Society of Operative Tobacconists

1837   First of the Tolpuddle Martyrs return to England

1838   Beginning of Chartism marked by publication of the People's Charter

1839   First Chartist national petition to Parliament

1842   General strike across the Midlands and North of England over wage cuts; Second Chartist national petition to Parliament

1845 National Association of United Trades formed as a trade union co-ordinating body; London Society of Compositors founded

1847 Ten Hours Act restricts working time for women and young people

1848 Third Chartist national petition presented to Parliament

1849 Typographical Association founded

1851 Amalgamated Society of Engineers formed – first of the 'New Model' unions

1854 Association of Correctors of the Press founded

1859 Building employers seek to introduce 'the document' forcing workers to give up union membership in response to campaign for nine-hour day, leading to six-month lockout and strike across London

1860 London Trades Council formed; emergence of the 'Junta' of London Trades Council leadership as de facto national leadership of the trade union movement; Amalgamated Society of Carpenters and Joiners founded; Coal Mine Regulations Act forbids the employment of boys under twelve years old underground

1866 Manchester Trades Council formed; In Hornby v Close, the courts rule that trade union funds are not protected against embezzlement under the Friendly Societies Act 1855, as trade unions remain illegal though not criminal bodies; Royal Commission on Trade Unions begins work following Sheffield 'outrages' in which a local union leader used gunpowder to blow up the house of a non-member

1867 Master and Servant Act liberalizes the law on conspiracy relating to wage earners' contract of service

1868 First meeting of the Trades Union Congress in Manchester, C W Bowerman becomes secretary to its parliamentary committee; Second Reform Act extends the franchise

1869 George Potter becomes secretary to the parliamentary committee of the TUC

1870 National Union of Elementary Teachers (later National Union of Teachers) founded

1871 Trade Union Act allows Registrar of Friendly Societies to register trade unions and provides a legal basis for their activities and protection for their funds; Criminal Law Amendment Act makes picketing a criminal offence; Amalgamated Society of Railway Servants founded

1872 Joseph Arch forms National Agricultural Labourers' Union; George Odger becomes secretary to the parliamentary committee of the TUC

1873 George Howell becomes secretary to the parliamentary committee of the TUC

1875 Conspiracy and Protection of Property Act legalizes picketing once again

1876 Trade Union Amendment Act protects union funds; Henry Broadhurst becomes secretary to the parliamentary committee of the TUC

1880 Associated Society of Locomotive Engineers and Firemen founded

1885 George Shipton becomes secretary to the parliamentary committee of the TUC

1886 Henry Broadhurst becomes secretary to the parliamentary committee of the TUC for the second time

1888 Miners' Federation formed; strike by matchgirls at Bryant & May factory in London's East End; first successful equal pay resolution at TUC conference

1889 London dock strike; gasworkers' strike; Electrical Trades Union formed; Postmen's Union formed

1890 Charles Fenwick becomes secretary to the parliamentary committee of the TUC

1894 Sam Woods becomes secretary to the parliamentary committee of the TUC

1895 TUC excludes trades councils from separate representation at congress

1896 Conciliation (Trades Disputes) Act empowers the Board of Trade to appoint conciliators and arbitrators in industrial disputes if asked to do so

1901 Taff Vale judgement makes union funds liable for damages caused by strikes

1905 W C Steadman becomes secretary to the parliamentary committee of the TUC; National Association of Local Government Officers founded

1906 National Federation of Women Workers formed; Trade Disputes Act reverses Taff Vale judgement; Labour Party formed with twenty-six MPs following general election

1909 Osborne judgement forbids unions to give financial support to Labour candidates; National Agricultural Labourers' and Rural Workers' Union founded

1911 Printers' strike leads to publication of *Daily Herald*; C W Bowerman becomes secretary to the parliamentary committee of the TUC

1913 National Union of Railwaymen formed; Trade Union Act gives unions the right to form separate political funds after a ballot, with individual members able to opt out

1914 TUC declares 'industrial truce' for duration of war

1915 Unofficial strikes by munitions workers on the Clyde; shop stewards' movement emerges in defiance of official TUC leadership's willingness to work with government in support of the war effort

1917 Trade Union Amalgamations Act makes mergers and amalgamations easier, leading to the creation of the Amalgamated Engineering Union (1920), Transport and General Workers' Union (1922) and National Union of General and Municipal Workers (1924); National Foremen's Association founded

1918 Fifty-seven Labour MPs elected in general election; National Union of Scientific Workers founded

1919 35 million days lost to strikes as industrial action sweeps many industries; Police Act bars police officers from joining a union or taking industrial action

1920   Amalgamated Engineering Union formed, bringing together ten engineering unions

1921   C W Bowerman becomes the first general secretary of the TUC when the general council replaces the parliamentary committee

1923   Fred Bramley becomes secretary of the TUC

1924   First minority Labour government takes office under James Ramsay MacDonald

1925   Walter Citrine becomes acting general secretary of the TUC, taking on the post permanently in 1926

1926   General strike over wage cuts in mining industry

1927   Trade Disputes Act forces civil service unions to leave the TUC and imposes restrictions on picketing; strike action in sympathy with workers in other industries made illegal

1929   Second minority Labour government elected under MacDonald; Labour the largest party with 288 MPs

1931   MacDonald and Snowden (Chancellor of the Exchequer) seek to cut unemployment benefits and public spending in response to poor economic situation, but are opposed by TUC general council and most cabinet ministers; Labour splits and general election leads to creation of National (Conservative) government under MacDonald

1939   Bridlington Agreement between TUC unions bans poaching of members

1942   Amalgamated Engineering Union admits women for first time, signing up 139,000 within a year

1943   In the wake of strikes by bus drivers and dock workers in Liverpool, Defence Regulation 1AA makes incitement to strikes illegal

1945   First majority Labour government elected; National Union of Mineworkers founded; World Federation of Trade Unions unites international union movement, but American Federation of Labor remains outside

1946   Repeal of Trades Disputes and Trade Unions Act 1927 allows civil service unions to affiliate to the TUC

1947 National Coal Board created on 1 January, taking coal industry into public ownership; Vincent Tewson becomes secretary of the TUC

1948 TUC and other Western European unions leave World Federation of Trade Unions to create International Confederation of Free Trade Unions while Soviet bloc unions remain in WFTU

1955 Engineers and electricians working on Fleet Street strike for three weeks, preventing publication of daily newspapers; train drivers in Associated Society of Locomotive Engineers and Firemen strike over pay claim

1956 Transport and General Workers' Union moves left with election of Frank Cousins as general secretary

1958 Congress House opens as headquarters of the TUC

1959 National Amalgamated Stevedores and Dockers union expelled from TUC after five-year dispute over the poaching of TGWU members; George Woodcock becomes general secretary of the TUC

1961 TUC expels Electrical Trades Union over allegations of ballot rigging, but is readmitted in 1962 after Communist leadership is ousted in fresh elections by right-wing grouping

1963 Contracts of Employment Act requires employers to give minimum period of notice

1964 Labour government elected under Harold Wilson

1965 Redundancy Payments Act requires consultation and compensation payments

1968 Royal Commission on Trade Unions (Donovan Commission) recommends continuation of self-regulation

1969 *In Place of Strife* white paper recommends statutory pre-strike ballots and improved recognition rights; Vic Feather becomes general secretary of the TUC

1971 Industrial Relations Act requires unions to register, and makes all collective agreements legally enforceable through an Industrial Relations Court

1972   Miners' strike; dock workers' strike

1973   Len Murray becomes general secretary of the TUC

1974   Miners' strike; Labour government elected (general elections in February and October) under Harold Wilson; Trade Union and Labour Relations Act replaces Industrial Relations Act; Health and Safety at Work Act passed

1975   Equal Pay Act requires employers to pay men and women the same rates for the same work

1978–79 Winter of discontent sees many public sector disputes

1980   Trade union membership peaks at 13 million

1980–93 Six Employment Acts restrict industrial action by requiring pre-strike ballots, outlawing secondary action, restricting picketing and giving employers the right to seek injunctions where there is doubt about the legality of action

1984   Norman Willis becomes general secretary of the TUC; year-long miners' strike over pit closures ends in defeat

1986   Print workers' dispute with Rupert Murdoch of News International ends in derecognition at News International

1993   John Monks becomes general secretary of the TUC; Unison created by merger of NALGO, National Union of Public Employees and Confederation of Health Service Employees

1997   Labour government elected under Tony Blair

1998   National Minimum Wage Act sets legal minimum rates

1999   Employment Relations Act introduces statutory right to trade union recognition where supported by a majority of the workforce (effective 2000)

2002   Merger between the Manufacturing, Science and Finance Union and the Amalgamated Electrical and Engineering Union creates Amicus

2003   Brendan Barber becomes general secretary of the TUC

2004   Banking union Unifi and Graphical, Paper and Media Union merge with Amicus

2005   Higher proportion of women than men in trade unions for
first time; number of days' work lost to industrial disputes at
lowest point on record

2007   Unite formed from amalgamation of Transport and General
Workers' Union with Amicus

BIBLIOGRAPHY

Books: General and Reference

Chase, Malcolm, *Early Trade Unionism: Fraternity, Skill and the Politics of Labour* (Ashgate, 2000)

Dictionary of Labour Biography, ed. John Saville and Joyce Bellamy (vols 1 to 10); David Howell, Neville Kirk and Keith Gildart (vols 11 and 12) (Macmillan, 1971–2004)

Gorman, John, *Banner Bright: An Illustrated History of Trade Union Banners* (Scorpion Publishing, new edition 1986)

Historical Directory of Trade Unions, Vol. 1: ed. A Marsh and V Ryan, *Non-manual unions* (Scolar Press, 1980)

    Vol. 2: ed. A Marsh and V Ryan, *Unions in engineering, shipbuilding and minor metal trades, coal mining and iron and steel, agriculture, fishing and chemicals* (Scolar Press, 1984)

    Vol. 3: ed. A Marsh and V Ryan, *Unions in building and allied trades, transport, woodworkers and allied trades, leather workers, enginemen and tobacco workers* (Gower Publishing, 1987)

    Vol. 4: ed. A Marsh, V Ryan and J Smethurst, *Unions in cotton, wool and worsted, linen and jute, silk, elastic web, lace and net, hosiery and knitwear, textile finishing, tailors and garment workers, hat and cap, carpets and textile engineering* (Scolar Press, 1994)

    Vol. 5: ed. A Marsh and J Smethurst, *Unions in printing and publishing, local government, retail and distribution, domestic services, general employment, financial services, agriculture* (Ashgate, 2006)

    Vol. 6: ed. J Smethurst and P Carter, *Unions in building and construction, agriculture, fishing, chemicals, wood and woodworking, transport, engineering and metal working, government, civil and public service, shipbuilding, energy and extraction* (Ashgate, 2009)

Leeson, R A, *United We Stand: An Illustrated Account of Trade Union Emblems* (Adams & Dart, 1971)

Prothero, Iorwerth, *Artisans and Politics in Early Nineteenth Century London: John Gast and His Times* (Wm Dawson & Son, 1979)

Reid, Alastair J, *United We Stand: A History of Britain's Trade Unions* (Penguin Books, 2005)

Southall, Humphrey, Gilbert, David and Bryce, Carol, *Nineteenth Century Trade Union Records: An Introduction and Select Guide* (Historical Geography Research Series, 1994)

Webb, Sidney and Beatrice, *The History of Trade Unionism 1666–1920* (2nd edition, 1920)

Books: Individual Unions

Burchill, Frank and Ross, Richard, *A History of the Potters' Union* (Ceramic and Allied Trades Union, 1977)

Coates, Ken and Topham, Tony, *The Making of the Labour Movement: The Formation of the Transport and General Workers' Union 1870–1922* (Spokesman, 1994)

Fox, Alan, *A History of the National Union of Boot and Shoe Operatives 1874–1957* (Basil Blackwell, 1958)

Fyrth, H J and Collins, Henry, *The Foundry Workers: A Trade Union History* (Amalgamated Union of Foundry Workers, 1959)

Groves, Reg, *Sharpen the Sickle! The History of the Farm Workers' Union* (Porcupine Press, 1959)

Higenbottam, S, *Our Society's History* (Amalgamated Society of Woodworkers, 1939)

Hoffmann, P C, *They Also Serve: The Story of the Shopworker* (Porcupine Press, 1949)

Hopwood, Edwin, *The Lancashire Weavers' Story: A History of the Lancashire Cotton Industry and the Amalgamated Weavers' Association* (Amalgamated Weavers' Association, 1968)

Marsh, Arthur and Ryan, Victoria, *The Clerks: A History of Apex 1890–1989* (Malthouse Publishing, 1997)

McKillop, Norman, *The Lighted Flame: A History of the Associated Society of Locomotive Engineers and Firemen* (Thomas Nelson & Sons, 1950)

Murray, Andrew, *The T & G story: A History of the Transport and General Workers' Union, 1922–2007* (Lawrence & Wishart, 2007)

Postgate, R W, *The Builders' History* (National Federation of Building Trade Operatives, 1923)

Pugh, Sir Arthur, *Men of Steel: A Chronicle of Eighty-eight Years of Trade Unionism* (Iron and Steel Trades Confederation, 1951)

Books: Strikes and Disputes

Jenkins, Mick, *The General Strike of 1842* (Lawrence & Wishart, 1980)

Perkins, Anne, *A Very British Strike: 3 May – 12 May, 1926* (Macmillan, 2006)

Books: Biography and Autobiography

Chapple, Frank, *Sparks Fly! A Trade Union Life* (Michael Joseph, 1984): autobiography of the electricians' union leader

Fishman, Nina, *Arthur Horner: A Political Biography* (Lawrence & Wishart, 2006): biography of the miners' union leader

Goldman, Harold, *Emma Paterson: She Led Women into a Man's World* (Lawrence & Wishart, 1974): biography of the nineteenth-century women workers' union leader

Jenkins, Clive, *All Against the Collar: Struggles of a White Collar Union Leader* (Methuen, 1990): autobiography of the office workers' union leader

Silver, Eric, *Victor Feather, TUC: A Biography* (Victor Gollancz, 1973): biography of the TUC leader

Sirs, Bill, *Hard Labour* (Sidgwick & Jackson, 1985): autobiography of the steelworkers' union leader

Stewart, Margaret, *Frank Cousins: A Study* (Hutchinson, 1968): biography of the TGWU leader

Thorne, Will, *My Life's Battles* (1st edn 1925; republished Lawrence & Wishart, 1989): autobiography of the gasworkers' union leader

Weighell, Sidney, *On the Rails* (Orbis Publishing, 1983): autobiography of the rail union leader

Books: Political Parties

Barltrop, Robert, *The Monument: The Story of the Socialist Party of Great Britain* (Pluto Press, 1976)

Bornstein, Sam and Richardson, Al, *Against the Stream: A History of the Trotskyist Movement in Britain 1924–38* (Socialist Platform, 1986)

Bornstein, Sam and Richardson, Al, *War and the International: A History of the Trotskyist Movement in Britain 1937–49* (Socialist Platform, 1986)

Eaden, James and Renton, Dave, *The Communist Party of Great Britain Since 1920* (Palgrave Macmillan, 2002)

Laybourn, Keith, *A Century of Labour: A History of the Labour Party, 1900–2000* (Sutton Publishing, 2001)

Morgan, Kevin, Cohen, Gidon and Flynn, Andrew, *Communists and*

British Society 1920–1991: People of a Special Mould (Rivers Oram Press, 2005)

Pelling, Henry and Reid, Alastair J, *A Short History of the British Labour Party* (Palgrave Macmillan, 2005)

Other Resources

Trade Union Badge Collectors Society

http://unionbadges.wordpress.com
Membership organization for collectors of trade union badges and ephemera. Publishes a bi-monthly newsletter and the magazine *Symbols of Solidarity*.

Society for the Study of Labour History

www.sslh.org.uk
Founded in 1960, the society is the UK's principal organization for the study of labour history, organizing events and publishing the academic journal *Labour History Review*.

Trade Union Ancestors

www.unionancestors.co.uk
Website for family historians produced by the author of this book. The site includes union 'family trees', a list of 5,000 historical unions and short histories of individual organizations, and links to further resources.

Chartist Ancestors

www.chartists.net
Website for family historians produced by the author of this book. The site includes many lists of Chartist activists, guides to further sources and information about the Chartist movement, including articles on links between the Chartists and the trade unions and on the 1842 general strike.

INDEX